The Afterlife Book

*because you never
got a chance to say goodbye*

Jeannie Reed

Skyhorse Publishing

Copyright © 2022 Jeannie Reed

All rights reserved. No part of this book may be reproduced in any manner without the express written consent of the publisher, except in the case of brief excerpts in critical reviews or articles. All inquiries should be addressed to Skyhorse Publishing, 307 West 36th Street, 11th Floor, New York, NY 10018.

Skyhorse Publishing books may be purchased in bulk at special discounts for sales promotion, corporate gifts, fund-raising, or educational purposes. Special editions can also be created to specifications. For details, contact the Special Sales Department, Skyhorse Publishing, 307 West 36th Street, 11th Floor, New York, NY 10018 or info@skyhorsepublishing.com.

Skyhorse® and Skyhorse Publishing® are registered trademarks of Skyhorse Publishing, Inc.®, a Delaware corporation.

Visit our website at www.skyhorsepublishing.com.
10 9 8 7 6 5 4 3 2 1

Library of Congress Cataloging-in-Publication Data is available on file.

Cover design by Kai Texel

Print ISBN: 978-1-5107-7051-5
Ebook ISBN: 978-1-5107-7052-2

Printed in the United States of America

for Dee and Bobby

Contents

Acknowledgments

I want to thank University of Virginia Reference Librarian Barbie Selby for her research on Dr. Ian Stevenson. I want to thank Marion Hedger for her "inside info" on Britain's Witchcraft Act of 1935 and its repeal in 1951. I want to thank Dr. Marvin Belsky for twenty-five years of support and encouragement and the loan of a book that changed my mind, and so changed my life. I want to thank my dear friend Alejandro Carosso, whose astonishing library has been an invaluable resource for the writing of this book. I want to thank the many beautiful, "ordinary" people who answered my craigslist posting and shared their *after*-death experience stories. I want to thank Dr. Carl Jung, Dr. Ian Stevenson, Dr. Brian Weiss, Dr. Raymond Moody, Jr., and Dr. Jim Tucker for believing enough to take the risk of putting us all before their own careers and reputations.

And I want to thank my family, friends, and clients for your support and encouragement over the years.

*Jesus said to her, "I am the resurrection
and the life. The one who believes in me
will live, even though they die."*

—John 11:25

It's not over.

—Jeffrey 9/20

Preface

I didn't know when I started this book where it could end up. All I can say is that in the three years' writing, miracles have been happening. And I've been able to capture much of it with a camera, clear as day. So clear that anybody looking at the pictures would have to say, "Yes! That is . . .".

I wrote this book for ordinary people. So that people can learn and know and understand the amazing world of spirit. I know now that many folks have been contacted by the loved ones they've lost. But too many don't know that. They don't know how to hear. They don't know how to listen. They've been told to be scared, so they've shut down.

And that's so sad.

At the beginning, I had an idea I could write a book about reincarnation. But no. Life took me in a very different direction. See, I've discovered that the spirit world is very much *with* us always. *ON this Earth, and in real time, and doing stuff all day long trying to get our attention!* As I said, I have pictures. And you've gotten messages. But maybe you don't know it. Yet.

This is such a big deal I can only hope I've done it justice. I hope I've said enough that people can say, wow! Because I just want folks to stop being afraid of dying.

Because I can say now that I *know* the spirit world is very much with us 24/7. If only we can all just accept that idea long enough to take an honest look. Many have done this and had the guts to write about it. Others have put their reputations on the line because they're able to accept brand-new ideas maybe not yet proven by science.

Because I want to give you a big picture of a subject that has a lot of moving parts, in this book you'll find Deepak Chopra, Plato, Dr. Carl Jung, Albert Einstein, the Delphic Oracle, Amedeo Modigliani, David Bohm, Michio Kaku, Carlo Rovelli. And Russell Targ and Werner Heisenberg and Abraham Lincoln and Socrates and Caroline Myss, and the rabbis and priests and mediums and philosophers and mystics and medical doctors who have researched and written about spirit life over many hundreds of years.

But here you'll also find the cab drivers and administrative assistants and teachers and executives among us right now . . . all with an afterlife story they're eager to tell.

And if you're asking yourself, *who is she to be writing about spiritualism and life after death?* Well, you'd better believe I've asked myself that question a lot in the past three years. All I can say is, first of all, I spent many years as a reporter. So, to do this book I figured I'd better put on my reporter's hat and start asking questions. I figured that if I didn't find solid answers, either I'd be the wrong person to be looking, or the answers I hoped for wouldn't be there at all.

And where did the idea come from in the first place to write about spirit life? Well, that was from the mystic part of me (yes, you have one too).

To put you in the picture:

* * *

July 1969.

It was the summer of Woodstock. It was the summer that marked "one small step for mankind." It was the summer I was struck by lightning as I walked along the roots of a towering maple at the end of the driveway. As the tree was falling behind me, I didn't know I was running for my life.

Three days later, I used an Aramaic word in a poem. *Atziluth.* And, of course, I thought the lightning had done something bad to my brain. I mean, this was a word I didn't know and had never learned. I thought it was jibberish that just came out of me. And I was scared that I was suddenly crazy. It would be at least twenty years before I'd learn that *it is actually a word* and that I'd used it correctly in the poem.

So, yes, it turns out that something *had* happened to me during that lightning strike. I had become psychic is all. It's as simple (and as complicated) as that.

Now I can look back and see that summer day was marking the beginning of a journey that has continued for fifty-two years.

I used to wonder: was I just some kind of happy psychic accident waiting to happen? Maybe was this lightning thing purely random?

After a lifetime of work in physics, Einstein would probably say . . . no. Not random. No way. But over time I've stopped wondering about this, and I've simply come to agree with him. Nothing in this world is random. Nothing in this world is chance. Nothing in this world is accidental. *Everything* is intended.

Now fast-forward to 1995.

* * *

I'd just moved into a little cottage in Barryville, New York, in a kind of isolated area on the side of a mountain. Down the road a bit was a place that had sure seen better days . . . like, maybe a hundred years before.

It happens that a three-generation family had just bought that place. And they were terrified. They said a hostile spirit was *punching holes* in a bedroom wall.

Well, by that time I was a professional psychic. So it came to pass that I was asked if I'd "take care" of the spirit.

Hunh? Certainly not! Talk about something being totally outside a job description!

But then I was told that having her own home was the grandmother's lifelong dream. And they were poor. And she was scared. So off I went. Out of compassion. It was a nice sunny summer morning.

Long story short, I'm pretty sure I managed to do what I set out to do that day: to encourage the angry spirit to go somewhere else ("the light") while not dying myself in the process. Once in the room, I encouraged the spirit to "go to the light." (Watch enough TV and this idea comes to mind pretty fast. Not that I have a clue even now if the idea is a real thing.)

Then I found myself praying The Lord's Prayer in my head and sobbing like crazy. It wasn't a plan. It just happened out of nowhere. (Of course, I was scared. I'd already discovered there was nothing *behind* the wall with the holes! No other room there . . . just the outside. And the punched-out plaster pieces were *inside*. Didn't take Columbo to figure this one out.) But at the time, I didn't know what I now know about spirits. Now I know that, mostly, they are love. So back then I was afraid.

And did this praying and urging thing turn out to be mission-accomplished at the old house?

Well, I never heard another scared word from that family. Thank God. Because you couldn't have made me go back to that dark and dingy third floor for all the tea in China.

(And let me say here: this was the first and last time I'll ever try anything like that, in daylight or not. I mean, all mediums are psychic. But not all psychics are mediums. And it's the mediums who do the spirit contact stuff.)

Anyway, I'm really hopeful that my visit that day marked the end of the eerie anger on the third floor and the terror of the occupants of that house. And I have to hope that a poor trapped soul finally found his way out, thanks a bit to me but mostly to God.

* * *

I tell these two stories because they stand out. Was there something pulling me (pushing me?) to the tree that day? Was there something pulling me (pushing me?) to live in the cottage just then?

These days, I think something *has* been pushing me all my life toward studying and talking about the very busy world of the afterlife and how it connects to us on Earth.

And that includes pushing me to a visit with a fine medium three years ago. A man who affirmed all that I'd started to think about my life that far.

And pushing me, finally, to not fear the artist who would come to teach me. The painter who's been in this apartment much of the time (I think) for six years now. Yes, he passed away in 1920. But as you'll see from the photos of the things he does, there's nothing hazy or vapory or un-real about him. He's as real as we are. He does real stuff with physical objects. Plus, he reads my mind . . . (And, look, this is me—an objective, scientific, careful person who's saying that.)

By the way? I have no idea *why* me, why now, why this. And maybe I never will. But I think we two, my painter and I, have something really important to share with you about life ever after. And that I'm supposed to be doing it.

So here goes.

Chapter One

Spiritualism: The Birth of a Movement

It is February 2021. The world has been in the grip of a killer virus for at least fourteen months. I see my Kips Bay librarian friend, Alicia, and I tell her about this book. She gets excited. She says, "This couldn't come at a better time. So many people have lost loved ones, and they never got a chance to say goodbye." And I hear this and realize the parallel: the very idea of mediumship and spirit contact reached its social heyday in this country because so many boys went off to the Civil War and never came back to so many families who grieved *because they never got a chance to say goodbye.*

So, thank you, Alicia. What you said the other day hadn't occurred to me. And it makes me really happy to think maybe this work can ease somebody's pain, as you imagine it. And also to think that maybe the acceptance of spiritualism in America has come full-circle.

* * *

I'd like to talk first of all about what the smithsonian.com website says about spiritualism: ". . . . the movement known as Modern Spiritualism sprang from several distinct revolutionary philosophies and characters. The ideas and practices of Franz Anton Mesmer, an

18th-century German healer, had spread to the United States and by the 1840s held the country in thrall. Mesmer proposed that everything in the universe, including the human body, was governed by a 'magnetic fluid' that could become imbalanced, causing illness. By waving his hands over a patient's body, he induced a 'mesmerized' hypnotic state that allowed him to manipulate the magnetic force and restore health. Amateur mesmerists became a popular attraction at parties and in parlors, a few proving skillful enough to attract paying customers. Some who awakened from a mesmeric trance claimed to have experienced visions of spirits from another dimension."

(Let me add here that in many places the words "spiritualism" and "spiritism" are used interchangeably. I prefer "spiritualism," so that's the word I use in this book.) Among those of us who do believe in life after death, there are many who feel that *between death and new life* the soul can be reached and communicated with. This belief has come to be called spiritualism. (This communication is what's been happening with me in this apartment for six years . . . so far.)

I've read that "the first" acknowledged modern spiritualist was Emanuel Swedenborg, the Lutheran theologian, scientist, and mystic. Like the ancient Greeks, he believed that the soul, the spirit, is eternal. This was in the mid-1700s in Europe. Centuries before him, the ancient Greek philosopher Socrates is said to have noted, "I am confident that there truly is such a thing as living again, that the living spring from the dead, and that the souls of the dead are in existence."

Clearly, whatever the truths, whatever has been lost in the mists of time, one thing is for sure: we don't know everything about death. I mean, suppose we only know half the story? Suppose we know even *less* than half? Yes, we see our bodies die, we see the color leave the skin, we see the eyes lose their shine, we see the breath and heartbeat cease. We see all that. We can measure all that with machines now, too. In some cases, we can even keep the body going with other machines.

But then what? At some point, we have to be done, right? And then we're left with the question: Is *that* all we are? What we *were*? Well, this makes no sense to me! All religions argue that we're more than flesh and bone. They also say we're even more than mind and thought. All religions believe that man is blessed with a soul, that this soul is our link to God, and so it must live forever, since God is eternal. And in some faith-based cultures, people see reincarnation as fact. They tell us—as Socrates and many others have believed over the centuries—they tell us that souls come back to new bodies after leaving used ones. Our souls.

If you'd like to explore the philosophical basis of the persistence of the soul after life, Dr. Deepak Chopra's *Life After Death* looks into the subject from many points of view. The author focuses on levels of consciousness beyond this one we know so well.

Rhine and Jung

In 1895, American J. B. Rhine founded the field of parapsychology as a branch of psychology. Rhine was an educator and botanist, a man of science and pragmatism, yet he couldn't believe that what we see is all we get. *Parapsychology* is defined by Webster, basically, as "the scientific study of events that cannot be explained by what scientists know about nature and the world." So, then, we can imagine that Rhine had imagination, courage, and vision. At least, I can imagine that.

Like the others before him, Rhine believed that the spirit survives beyond death and can be communicated with. But when his work couldn't lead him to that conclusion in a *scientific* way, he turned to parapsychology research.

I have to say this must've been an enormous leap of faith for a college professor, especially back then. Imagine one of your own teachers today, mostly married to his/her dogma, deciding to climb out on that hazardous limb and risk the reactions of peers and the school! I suspect tenure would become hard to acquire for those brave folks, when it's my experience with academia so far that it toes a *very* conservative line.

So I say we owe this man, Rhine, a huge debt of gratitude for putting his neck on the line like that and getting the psychic ball rolling in this usually backward-looking country, America. I'm pretty sure not all his colleagues would've thought he was in his right mind. It's ironic when you think about it. This nation was founded by a bunch of renegades, but just let one come along today and threaten to disrupt the status quo . . .

Meanwhile, at pretty much the same time that Rhine was working on his own ideas, Swiss psychiatrist Dr. Carl Jung was exploring his theory about a "universal unconsciousness" as a level of brain activity. (It's thanks to the work and the courage of Jung—who explored the tarot and astrology and the *I Ching*, among other occult devices—that I finally got brave enough to look deep into these things myself. See, at heart I try to think like a scientist, always looking for proof. And in a way, for the last forty years I guess I'd have to say that my life has been my laboratory. Being a respected scientist, Dr. Jung became for me a credible, respectable bridge between spirit and matter, between the universal connectedness of all people and the ground on which they walk. That is to say: a bridge between me and the great unknown.)

If you'd like to know more about Jung and spiritualism, there are several articles in older issues of *The Journal of Religion and Psychical Research* about Dr. Jung and his slow conversion to the acceptance of spirit activity in our daily humdrum lives.

Spiritualism

But even before Rhine and Jung and others of their turn of mind started digging into this stuff of spirit as *science*, things were happening. Thanks to the mediumistic work of Kate and Margaret Fox, the year 1848 saw the birth of spiritualism in the United States as a *religious* movement. Churches were founded dedicated to the philosophy. Experiments were conducted. Teachings were sent far and wide. Bogus "spiritualists" appeared, of course, and were exposed in due course. While at the same time, critics totally pooh-poohed the whole "crazy" idea that we can hear from the dead, never mind speak with them. And so, mainstream society pretty much ended up throwing the baby out with the bath water.

Then, as now, spiritualists believed that the soul after death can communicate with the living—a phenomenon akin to what Rhine was talking about. Many methods were devised to attempt this feat. Many are in use to this day. In fact, it seems to me that, in the last fifteen years or so, America is experiencing a renaissance of spiritualist practices.

(Two long-popular tools that come to mind for facilitating spirit communication are the Ouija board and automatic writing. In both cases, the person doing the thing seems to have no control over what's happening.)

The historical fact is that the "modern" heyday of spiritualism, its so-called Golden Age, was the last half of the 1800s into the early 1900s. During this time, mainly among the wealthy and privileged, spiritualism became a kind of social force. And in Western cultures, societies were formed around the idea. In 1882, for example, the Society for Psychical Research was founded in London, England, and in the same time period, so-called spiritualist "camps" cropped up in the United States. Among these have been Lily Dale Assembly, Lily Dale, New York (which still functions); Camp Silver Belle, Ephrata, Pennsylvania (an active spiritualist summer camp until 1976); Camp Chesterfield, in Indiana (founded in 1886 and functioning still); and Camp Cassadaga, Lake Helen, Florida (in use today and since the late 1800s as a place of spiritualist practice, worship, and instruction). These may be the best known in the United States—particularly Lily Dale and Cassadaga—but there are no doubt smaller, less well-known spiritualist churches cropping up now across the landscape. I think this because the United States seems to be experiencing a rebirth of interest in spiritualism and in mysticism in general. I wonder if this interest will ever grow as strong as it was here in the second half of the 19th century . . . well, I hope so.

At the time of the heyday, there were also a few publications dedicated to mediumship and spiritualism, among them *Mind and Matter* and *Herald of Progress*. There was *Spiritual Age*, which entered the political arena when it urged its readers to vote for Wisconsin Territory Governor Nathaniel Tallmadge for president, because he was a spiritualist and reported to be a psychic as well. There was *Banner of Light*, a spiritualist newspaper that published a section of "messages" from dead soldiers to their loved ones left behind. These were in the United States.

In Britain, among others, there were *Spiritual Magazine*, the *Spiritualist*, and the *Medium*.

Meanwhile, British writer Sir Arthur Conan Doyle (who created Sherlock Holmes) had become a major booster of the spiritualist movement and philosophy. He knew his reputation would take a hit if he went public with this, but the man had the courage to do it anyway. In an interview reported by *The Medium's Medium* (a journal published by London's The Gallery of Everything), Doyle was asked *the* question: "Can one be a spiritualist and also a Christian?" He replied, "Spiritualism is not incompatible with any religion. It is only hostile to those creeds which would confine God's mercy to a particular sect. He is the God of all." Still, despite the fact that Doyle held such moderate views, he did take a hit. His reputation reportedly sank to some kind of new low in 1920 (though his brilliant Holmes thrives to this day).

Then there was France: more specifically, Paris at the turn of the 20th century.

As I was doing research into the painter, Modigliani, I made a discovery. In the first couple of decades of the 20th century, Paris, France, was the center of a high point of spiritualism. It's believed that poet William Blake and his metaphysical ideas were the source of the interest, which was huge among the artists and writers of Montmartre. I've learned that among the great painters who attended séances and consulted with psychics, spiritual principles became significant in their work. Among these were Modigliani, pioneer Hilma af Klint (*Paintings for the Temple*), Pablo Picasso (painting: *Fortune Teller*), Ernst Josephson (who would have been in at the start of the cultural movement), Augustin Lesage (described by biographer Maximillien De Lafayette as "the greatest spirit and medium artist of all time"), Madge Gill, Fleury-Joseph Crepin, Max Jacob (artist and astrologer), Piet Mondrian, and Wassily Kandinsky. I imagine there were others, but these are the painters whose names I've found so far, connected with the spiritualism movement. Writer Victor Hugo (*The Hunchback of Notre Dame*) was also influenced by the movement in Paris in the early 20th century.

More recently: London's The Gallery of Everything staged an art exhibit in 2019 called "The Medium's Medium" (*Spiritualist*

Art Practices from the Turn of the Century and Beyond). The gallery lists pieces in this show by Marian Spore Bush, Margarethe Held, Marguerite Burnat-Provins, Emma Kunz, Georgiana Houghton, Hilma af Klint . . . and, you know, I suddenly have to wonder where the men are!!

(Look to this gallery as well for a collection of spirit photographs.)

Outside Western Europe and America during that time, we find spiritualism taking hold as well. During the reign of Tsar Nicholas I (the first half of the 19th century), Russian society became interested in mediums and séances. *The Journal of Religion and Psychical Research* reports that "the contrast between the rise of spiritualism in society and literature with the puritanic interests of Nicholas' court was unusual." We're told, "It is possible that spiritualism satisfied elements of the public's spiritual and intellectual needs which the rigid and dogmatic Russian church could not satisfy." But when the new tsar, Alexander II, arrived to rule the country during the second half of the 19th century, Russia found itself in the hands of a ruler who was "fascinated by the occult science and had séances in the Winter Palace." I take from this that the people of Tsarist Russia were just as spiritually needy as those in late 19th-century Western Europe and America. And they too were seeking some kind of solace in believing they could communicate with their deceased loved ones.

Harry Houdini

Meanwhile, back in America:

Curiously, in 1920, the very year that Sir Arthur Conan Doyle's public persona started to lose its shine, one of the most famous scoffers ever took the bit in his teeth and went after spiritualism. This was the year that the great American magician Harry Houdini became interested in the occult world. He'd lost his mother, Cecilia, seven years before and became involved with psychic phenomena soon after, when he thought he might be able to contact her through mediums. But of course, he found himself coming up against a ton of "spiritual charlatanism"—in other words, he was meeting a lot of people who claimed to be able to contact her but who were really frauds. I have no doubt that most of the "psychics" he encountered in his quest *were* in fact bogus (as is the case today), and so he abandoned his seeking and became hell-bent on exposing the frauds.

After a time, Houdini started working this material into his own act. It seems he started creating stage illusions . . . to dispel illusions of a different sort. He also recorded his experiences in a book, *A Magician Among the Spirits*.

After all this, though, Houdini didn't just throw the baby out with the bath water. He maintained a solid belief in something beyond this life. He made a deal with his wife, Bess, that after his death he would contact her with a coded message if he could. Bess started holding séances for this purpose in 1927, the year Houdini died. The last séance was held in 1936. But success eluded her.

I have to say here that I think what Houdini did was good. I think skepticism can be a very good thing. See, everything we're asked to take on faith is something we can be seduced by (and not in a fun way). Which means to me that anybody who has doubts while retaining an open mind is thinking right.

Abraham Lincoln: Then

During the 1860s, at what was essentially the starting point for the Golden Age of spiritualism, America was wracked by war. The Civil War was taking our young men at a horrendous rate on both sides of the conflict. Brother pitted against brother. North against South. And expected to preside over this bloody calamity with sense and strategy was the commander-in-chief, the 16th United States president, Abraham Lincoln.

Presidential historian Doris Kearns Goodwin tells us in *Team of Rivals: The Political Genius of Abraham Lincoln*: "Spiritualism would reach epic proportions during the Civil War, fueled perhaps by the overwhelming casualties." A Union army officer's wife, Agnes Elizabeth W. Salm-Salm, tells us, "The spiritualist epidemic was then commencing to rage in America. One heard of nothing but of spirits and mediums. All tables and other furniture seemed to have become alive, and you could not sit down upon a chair without a spiritual suspicion." And Civil War scholar Ernest B. Furguson notes: "This was not a superstition restricted to slave and servants; it is said that prominent Boston intellectuals, European royalty, men as hardheaded as [politician, soldier, and diplomat] Daniel Sickles and [US Navy Secretary] Gideon Welles sought to contact the dear departed in séances presided over by mediums who claimed the magic touch." And historian Margaret Leech tells us: "Spiritualism, the accompaniment of long and wasting wars, was rampant in the capital in the third winter of conflict. People sat hand-in-hand around tables in the dark, to hear bells rung and drums thumped and banjos twanged." I guess that because hope was in such short supply during those war years, desperate people looked for solace however they could, just as many do today.

(I have to note here that I couldn't find first-hand the 1860s writings referenced above and had to rely on Internet reports.)

So then, those terrible Civil War years formed the social environment in which the 16th US president and his wife found themselves after the tragic death of their own son, Willie. Wife Mary was said to be emotionally destroyed by the loss, while a grieving President Lincoln still had to deal with the horror that was the Civil War and all the death and bloodshed it was bringing.

Putting aside the talk of frauds for a second, it is history that the First Lady, Mary Todd Lincoln, believed very much in the work of the spiritualists. It's said she was desperate to reconnect with her boy, as any loving mother might be, and that she was looking wherever she could for this to happen.

They say it's reported in the National First Ladies Library: "Responding to the loss as Jane Pierce had previously to her own, Mary Lincoln began consulting a series of mediums, attending the séance circles of Cranston Laurie, and inviting Nettie Colburn Maynard, William Shockle [sic] and another identified in the historical record only as 'Colchester of Georgetown' to conduct these 'calls to the dead'—in the White House Red Room."

The mention here of Jane Pierce has to do with the fact that President Franklin Pierce's wife is also known to have invited mediums to the White House to connect with her own dead son, Bennie. This means that Mary Lincoln wouldn't have been the first White House resident to look to spiritualists to ease the pain of loss. In particular, we're told the First Lady turned mostly to Nettie Maynard, then a quite fashionable medium in Washington, D.C. circles.

And despite the fact that we have only Nettie's word (in a memoir) that there was any kind of spiritualistic relationship between her and President Lincoln, such a story persists even now. The story goes that President Lincoln attended at least one séance in the White House, and as *Maynard* claims, she was able to help him *politically* more than once. (Note: I find *no* supporting evidence for this claim of hers.)

I want to say something here. Something quite unexpected happened when I started looking into the idea of Lincoln reaching out to mediums to connect with the spirit of his dead son. Frankly, there's absolutely no reliable source or proof for these claims, although they do make juicy stories, Lincoln being the president and all. But I take from the rampant stories that circulated at the time, and from some that persist to this day—well, I take it that the fact that such stories have lasted over so many years is simply a testament to the persistence of the *idea* itself. It's clear to me that when things got so bold as to include the President of the United States, the hold of spiritualism must have been solid in those days. Clearly, that belief system seems to have had a big hold at the time on Washington, D.C. and on New York society. For me, the fact that a tale is repeated anywhere *a hundred and fifty years later* has to be at least a testament to the pull of the *idea* behind it (even if the story itself turns out to be a total crock). People at the time did believe.

For a modern-day example: look today at the persistence of psychic phone lines for several decades now. And I'm pretty sure that most of the people on the other end of those phone lines aren't in any way psychic. Yet callers are willing to pay as much as a dollar a minute to speak with them, because the callers want so badly to believe. And this is even *after* the fraudulent "Miss Cleo" was nailed as a charlatan and the whole phone line thing was blown wide open several years ago. Still, some people out there know that psychic phenomena *do* exist and that not all folks are frauds. So even after the Cleos of the world mess with its credibility, the demand for psychic work continues.

Plus, we *want* so much to believe in the "magic."

Yes, there's also that . . . the magic.

As for Lincoln in his day, no doubt most practical people would've thought the president quite foolish to go anywhere near a spiritualist and a séance. It would've been such ammunition for his political foes. His credibility would've been shredded for it. (I think even I would've been one of those practical types questioning the capabilities of such a president.) Still, I can imagine a stressed-out, grieving father wishing desperately that just for one more brief second he could reconnect with the little boy he'd lost. It's just not beyond the realm of reason for me to think the man may have reached out. For solace. But in secret, of course. We can't be having national leaders believing in ghosts, now can we?

So today I'm left to wonder. True? Not true? Lincoln's faith in the mystical was such that he'd participate in a séance? Fantasy, or the real deal? I do admit that since the 1860s, social norms have changed quite a bit, and I do have quite an imagination. Still, I just can't go so far as to imagine this thoughtful and serious man riding gleefully on a floating piano, as was reported some years after his death. Though I *can* imagine him thinking there might be more to life than "this," especially after the death of his boy and amid the ruinous horror of the Civil War. And I have no problem thinking about such a gentle man looking for answers in such dangerous and uncharted territory.

As for today:

Remember? In 1963, psychic Jeane Dixon predicted the assassination of President John Kennedy. There were witnesses to the prediction. Her friends say it really did something to her that she had no way to warn him—and this sadness she had to live with for the rest of her life.

Then there was General George Patton. They say this man could smell the blood in a place where there had once been a battle and that he believed in forces that we can't see or explain and that we need to pay attention because otherwise we are doomed to fail.

Then there is Benjamin Franklin, who reportedly said that he regarded death to be as necessary to good health as sleep. We're told he believed that after death we rise again, refreshed. In other words,

Franklin's belief was that that he would exist, in one shape or another, forever.

And some of you will remember that the news media had a field day when it was discovered First Lady Nancy Reagan "believed in" astrology, after her husband, President Ronald Reagan, was shot in an assassination attempt on March 30, 1981. I figure she was desperate for some kind of reassurance that it couldn't happen again, so she turned to the stars . . . According to Sam Roberts in his terrific book, *Grand Central*, after the attempt on her husband's life the former First Lady " . . . relied on astrological advice to arrange the president's schedule."

Then there were the claims alleging that Hillary Clinton was "channeling" Eleanor Roosevelt when she visited Dr. Jean Houston to participate in what were in fact psychological exercises, when it was actually a "What would Eleanor do?" kind of thing. (And once again, now as then, I guess it just doesn't "do" to give the opposing political party any kind of ammunition that can be used to damage your credibility. Especially not if you're the wife of the president of the United States.)

By the way, though, a little note here about females: the idea of the *wives* of the US presidents being far more open to mystical things than their men tracks with my own experience for three decades as a professional psychic. By far, maybe more than ninety percent of my clients have been female, as have all but two of my several long-time students.

So I have to wonder if there's a kind of prejudice at work. Forgetting down-and-dirty political tricks for a minute, is it really that we all hate to think of our elected leaders as having weaknesses and flaws? Is it that we *need* to think they're perfect? If so, that's not okay for me. I have to think that ordinary people raised to exceptional positions are still, at heart, ordinary people. I mean, they don't magically become superman when they arrive in the nation's capital, right? Plus, isn't this the very core premise of democracy: that *anybody* "can be president"?

Of course, I also know for certain that the *other* half of that equation is equally true: regardless of what some people think, the supernatural *is* with us 24/7, and events *do* happen that defy logical explanation, and belief in that is totally right-on. My own beliefs were ridiculed for a long time by friends and colleagues but are now proved right-on. Well, at least to me they are.

Thankfully, headway in terms of mainstream acceptance is being made now. Sure, it's happening a bit at a time, but there are now dozens of books on the shelves dealing with mystical things like tarot and astrology and palmistry and the spirit world. It's no longer generally regarded as ridiculous in many circles today to "believe in" things we cannot see, taste, touch, feel, smell. (Yes, organized religions do teach this, but they call it "faith.")

Bottom line? I think it's not so much the "weakness" of the people we elect that we're dealing with here, it's the fact that we *call* them weak whenever they drift toward the mystical. And *that* is just plain prejudice. I can name a few national leaders right now who would greatly benefit the country if only their hearts and minds were open enough to understand that we live, we die, we live again. That kind of thing can get a person thinking!

Abraham Lincoln: Now
Okay, now for the new stuff. Well, new to me, anyway, because when I set out to look for evidence that Abraham Lincoln consorted with mediums and partook of the plenty of the spirit world, I never expected *this*.

I never expected that it would be Lincoln's *own* spirit that people would be reporting, from shortly after his death and into modern times. Most sightings so far have taken place in the White House. And this is something I hadn't heard before. (Looks like a White House tour may be in my future!)

Anyway, what I've learned—recorded here with huge gratitude to author Adam Selzer's fabulous research and book, *Ghosts of Lincoln*—is that over the years there have been various sightings of this amazing president. These have been made by many we'd all consider credible. Carl Sandburg, the poet, felt Lincoln's presence in the White House in a particular room at a particular window. Eleanor Roosevelt reported that several employees saw Lincoln's ghost staring out the same window. Queen Wilhemina of the Netherlands claimed to have seen Lincoln's ghost during a 1942 visit to the White House. President Reagan's daughter, Maureen, and husband Dennis Revell reported an "aura" that would appear at Lincoln's bed in the middle of the night. White House staffers for years, and maybe still, were telling people that Lincoln has a habit of wandering the upstairs halls. President Harry Truman, on the Edward R. Murrow TV show, attributed the source of mysterious footsteps from time to time to Lincoln walking around in the White House. [Okay, so I don't know if he was joking here, but even if he was, the *idea* of a Lincoln spirit didn't come to him out of nowhere. The reporter was aware of the story, for sure.] And White House staffers told Nancy Reagan that both President Eisenhower and British PM Winston Churchill saw Lincoln's ghost in the White House.

And now to something also really cool: Ford's Theatre, where Lincoln was assassinated on the night of April 14, 1865, is said to be haunted to this day, and most believe it's the spirit of Lincoln.

Selzer tells us that on April 14, 1975, actor Billy Dee Williams was there doing a memorial to Martin Luther King, Jr. and was interrupted by the sound of somebody running across the stage. But nobody was there. (Okay, this could be the spirit of John Wilkes Booth, the president's assassin, who jumped to the stage and ran. Then again, spirit manifestation is spirit manifestation, right? We don't have to like the person who shows up.)

Then, in the early 1980s, actor Hal Holbrook said he "felt a presence" in that theater, one that made him mess up his lines, a presence of "something coming from the Lincoln box."

On another occasion, during a gospel musical presentation, an actress is reported to have complained at intermission that whoever was shining a light from the box was distracting her. (There was nobody in the box.)

Then there are the stories about the "mysterious lights" said to pop on and off in the president's box at that theater.

And we also have the story of the tour guide who went to the third floor of the theater one day to raise the flag and was terrified by footsteps and jangling keys. But was anybody there? Nope.

The bottom line here is that I set out to look into the spirits around Lincoln and have ended up being totally involved with the spirit *of* Lincoln!

So, I recommend Selzer's book: there's a lot of the history of the time, which provides good context for the Lincoln "ghost" stories, and there are detailed retellings of the stories themselves. And as with other writers on mystical subjects, I totally appreciate that this author also hasn't bought into the bunch of Lincoln ghost tales that are clearly bogus. As I said, it's one thing to have an open mind. It's quite another to let just anything pour into it without giving it a second thought.

(And by the way, maybe we shouldn't read too much into this either, but both President Johnson and President Nixon are said to have declined invitations to this particular theater.)

As for other leaders we can put in the wow! category:

Henry Ford is quoted as saying, "I adopted the theory of reincarnation when I was 26. Genius is experience. Some seem to think it is a gift or talent, but it is the fruit of long experience in many lives."

And French emperor Napoleon Bonaparte believed he'd been born more than once. It's reported that he used to discuss with his generals who he'd been in a previous life.

Blithe Spirits

Ford's Theatre doesn't have a monopoly on spirit sightings, though. Not by a long shot. And I suspect I haven't found half the examples out there over the years. The June 23, 2019 issue of the *New York Post* features a story by Zachary Kussin, who gives us a round-up of tales of famous hauntings just around the borough of Manhattan.

He tells us about Olive Thomas, a Ziegfield Follies showgirl who died in Paris in 1920 on her honeymoon and in 1997 terrified a security guard at Broadway's New Amsterdam Theatre. She appeared, moved across the stage, and blew him a kiss before disappearing through a wall.

Kussin also tells us about speculation that it's an old Vaudeville performer, Al Kelly, who's now said to be haunting The Friars Club.

And he tells us about the Algonquin Hotel, whose Round Table lunches put the place on the map. This is the hotel in the history books, *the* place where the literary lions of the day came to shoot the breeze. He says, "Since [Dorothy] Parker's 1967 death . . . Algonquin guests have heard the sound of furniture moving within rooms and mysterious songs playing in the elevator." He quotes longtime hotel resident, Elise Gainer, as saying, "Objects appear and disappear . . . people have seen apparitions," including "the full-bodied apparition of Dorothy in the lobby area." Gainer's own book, *Ghosts and Murders of Manhattan*, strikes me as something I'd want to read.

Kussin also tells us that *The Sopranos* actor Michael Imperioli lived at the Hotel Chelsea for two months. One night in 1996, he says he had a "chilling encounter" there with a ghost most people take to be a woman named Mary (among others people say they've seen at the hotel). The author tells us that Imperioli spotted Mary at the end of a hallway, "kind of hunched over—her head was down, she was crying." He called to her to ask if she was okay, at which point a light bulb "popped' behind him, the hallway was cast in darkness, and when [he] looked back, the woman was gone.

Finally, Kussin tells us that people believe they've seen and interacted with the spirit of Dylan Thomas, the brilliant Welsh poet who drank himself to death at The White Horse Tavern in 1953. Some report him sitting at the bar one second and in the next . . . gone.

And Elsewhere Across America
The October 18, 2017 issue of *Forbes* magazine provides a long list of America's "haunted" hotels. Here are the top ten, for you adventurous travelers out there:

The Stanley, Estes Park, Colorado
Concord's Colonial Inn, Concord, Massachusetts
Admiral Fell Inn, Baltimore, Maryland
The Red Lion, Stockbridge, Massachusetts
Hanover Inn Dartmouth, Hanover, New Hampshire
Omni Parker House, Boston, Massachusetts
The Sagamore, Bolton Landing, New York
1886 Crescent Hotel & Spa, Eureka Springs, Arkansas

Hotel Monteleone, New Orleans, Louisiana
Jekyll Island Club Resort, Jekyll Island, Georgia

Meanwhile, *Travel & Leisure* magazine, September 2020 issue, names some of the same hotels and adds the *RMS Queen Mary*, dry-docked permanently in Long Beach, California, and (the very pink!) The Don Cesar on the Gulf of Mexico in St. Petersburg, Florida.

Spiritualism in a Modern World at War
So now I look around at what's happening around the globe today. I look at the terrorism and the unspeakable cruelty of certain radical groups. I look at the internal racial divides that plague nations even today. I look at the incredible lust for money that seems to drive too many people at the peril of too many other people . . . Well, I look at all this and I can't help but think that spiritualism can't come soon enough to be all over the place.

I mean, if we believe in the eternal life of the soul; if we believe that there are more important, vital things than money and material stuff; if we believe that we can't just do whatever we want to whoever we want and get away with it *forever* . . . then maybe we all get just a little bit more compassionate, if nothing else? Maybe we all get a little more thoughtful about how we act and what we do and whom we do it to?

See, I know that my own recent experiences with the supernatural have changed me. Or maybe all that has happened to me has simply brought out the "real" me, finally? Or maybe, I have to wonder, it's a little bit of both?

Whatever the source of the change in me, I know that I always think twice now about saying a hurtful word, about making a careless rejection, about ignoring the feelings of any other person in a relentless pursuit to get what I want. And there's also this: when I stop to think about what's possible in this amazing universe of ours, all of a sudden, my own stupid little stuff, my greedy little ambitions, seem to pale in comparison. It's like being bothered by some nagging little thing and looking up at the vast and endless universe on a brilliantly starry night. And that little thing shrinks, becoming like a single drop in a vast ocean. And for some reason I feel better.

So, then, does a belief in spirits, spiritualism in any form, take us down the road to a kind of purity, take us to love?

Yes, maybe that's it.

I hope.

Chapter Two

Science and the Unseen World

Now I have to tell you: I was pretty darn nervous when I discovered I couldn't get out of high school (never mind college) without taking science courses. Because the way scientists think just isn't the way my own mind works. For sure, I need proof of a lot of things in this life. But figuring out how to *get* it? Forget it! I've always been a "word" person. But words don't make the world go 'round. (I still think TV is some kind of magic. I mean, pictures coming through a wire?) So, yes, some of the stuff in this chapter is hard to understand. But you don't need to understand it any more than I do. I think we all just need to know that this stuff *exists*, and some of it is mind-blowing, and it isn't even the end of the road yet. And how do I know that? You'll see. Because *that* is the entire purpose of this book. To share *physical* proof of the spiritual, something we may never be able to see anywhere else.

Albert Einstein

Now I want to take you where most of you probably don't usually go.

I want to take you to the world of modern physics and the thinking of scientists like Albert Einstein. Maybe you know of his theory, e = mc²? They teach this General Theory of Relativity in school to help us to see that neither matter (m) nor energy (e) can be created or destroyed.

Webster's tells us that *matter* is "the substance of which a physical object is composed." Energy, on the other hand, is not physical in the same way. A light bulb is matter, but electricity and light are energy. *We* are matter. *We* are also energy waiting to happen.

The brilliant Einstein also said that randomness is not a possibility. He even noted at one point, "God does not play dice with the universe." In other words, nothing happens by accident. Not the orbits of the planets, not the construction of the atom, not the speed at which the molecules in our bodies zoom around (or don't), to keep us from kind of falling apart. Wait! Not even the "chance" first meeting of two lovers? Well, look, if nothing is random, and everything is meant to be, and I believe it is? Then not even that meeting is by chance.

So, the things to remember here are: one, *we cannot be created or destroyed.* On Earth, we are matter. And after that? Well, after that, if Einstein is right, we must be energy. And either way, on Earth or not, we must be *somewhere.* And two, we're not here by chance, here in this life.

String Theory

It's also modern science that has this incredible idea that everything in the universe is connected by invisible "strings"—that is to say, vibrating strings of energy. This idea is called string theory, and it's part of what I think happens when I do a tarot reading: I'm connected to my client by invisible "strings." And my client and I are both connected to the universe by these invisible "strings." Because of this, I can know what's in my client's head and heart somehow, because we're connected. Simple as that. And, no, I don't really understand the science of this, but I do believe it. There has to be a logical, *scientific* reason for psychic stuff to work, and I think this is part of it.

Dr. Michio Kaku

As I write this, Dr. Michio Kaku is a professor of theoretical physics at City College of New York. You might recognize him from his work on the History Channel, the BBC, the Discovery Channel, and the Science channel. He's the author of a great many books, including the newest one, *The God Equation*. I find his energy and passion inspiring and infectious! I love to listen to this guy on TV when he's talking about his favorite subject. His students are totally lucky to be able to study with him. Totally.

For the last five decades, Kaku's passion has been string theory, the idea that tells us we're all connected. No, we can't see the connections, but we do know a few things about them. For example, if we divide in two something even smaller than an atom, and we send the two parts far from each other, when we do something to one part, *the other part will feel it instantly*. This idea is described as entanglement. And whether you like it or not, you're entangled . . . even with your worst enemy!

As for *The God Equation*: this is a really smart book, elegant, even laugh-out-loud funny in places. In this book, Kaku writes: "The universe is a symphony." Well, if that's the case, *The God Equation* is one heck of an arpeggio. And, look, I know very little about science, and even less about math. Scientists like Dr. Kaku live in a world of numbers: they *live* to be able to prove the universe in a line of math just an inch long. They *live* to ask questions. The funny thing is, so do I. Which is how I ended up at string theory long ago, to explain how I can do what I can do as a psychic. I mean, if we're not all connected, I will forever get nowhere and my clients will be better off if I'm driving an Uber. But we *are* connected. There is no doubt. And Dr. Kaku has devoted five decades of his life to proving it.

Actually, I mention a few examples of this connectedness even after death in my book, *The Language of Tarot*. A child is killed far from home. The mother knows *in that moment*. No doubt about it. A soldier dies in a war far from home. The mother knows *in that moment*. A twin suffers an injury, accident or death, and the other twin knows it. The phone is about to ring and you know it, *and you know who's calling*. You just know.

This is the power of being connected, alive or dead. And I believe it exists because all those "strings" exist that people in science are telling us about. Look, it's not a coincidence that you think of a person and then that person calls. I don't care how many people want to think it's just chance. It's not! Ask Einstein.

Or you can ask physicist Carlo Rovelli, who tells us in the brilliant and beautiful *Helgoland* that entanglement ". . . is a phenomenon by which distant objects speak to each other from afar . . . like two lovers who guess each other's thoughts." He goes even further, though, to say that for entanglement a *third* object is necessary (to enable the two distant objects to relate). Or as he puts it, entanglement is "a dance for three."

Yes! And I say that the third thing in this dance is strings. And that two people can be sitting on the same couch at the same time, simply *knowing* each other's thoughts. Because there is nothing *but* connection between them! In fact, a second-century Buddhist, Nagarjuna, tells us that there is nothing that exists in itself independently from something else. And this philosopher knew it *nineteen hundred* years ago!

So, with all this in mind, it isn't too much of a leap (at least for me) to decide that if matter (people) cannot be created or destroyed, and if space and time don't exist on their own, then we must continue to be entangled *after* death. (And Mr. Rovelli will be pleased to know I have "observables" for this. *Physical* proof. Here. In this book.) I want to say that what I'm trying to do here is just to set the stage for you. Whether we ever meet, whether we ever even know each other's names, *we are connected.*

It was a Harvard University scientist named Andrew Strominger who first proposed string theory. This was in the early 1980s. But even then, the idea had been bouncing around for a long time. Remember the "ether" of the ancients? The Greek philosopher Aristotle thought that maybe light can travel from the sun to us because there's an invisible substance that carries it. He called that substance *ether*. (Not to be confused with the anesthetic.)

In modern times, though, there are more advanced and informed ideas about this "ether." And the new word for the connection concept these days is "strings." (I do have to mention here, this is a *theory*. So far, to my knowledge nobody has been able to prove in a science lab that "strings" exist one way or another. So until somebody does, it will stay a theory. Then again, gravity is a theory too, and so far, it works every time or we'd all be floating around above the ground and out of control.)

But for me there's no doubt about it. I'm with Kaku and the "string" people.

Take this one step further. As noted in the amazing book, *Tao Science*, Albert Einstein described the results of something called quantum entanglement as "mysterious (spooky) action at a distance." The basis for this statement is the idea that we are all tiny particle waves, and *distance does not affect communication between us.*

One idea of quantum entanglement was proposed by theoretical physicist Richard Feynman. His idea was that particles smaller than an atom can send information at great speeds, and *the brain* is the receiver. (This is in the same way that a network broadcasts a TV show, and your cable box receives it.) Feynman believed the brain can instantly receive information from both the past and the future. (This is all rather simple, I know. I just want you to know the thinking right now. If you want to know more, it's all out there! But as I said, I believe this is why psychics and mediums can work successfully.)

Sidney Dillon Emeritus Professor of Astronomy George Greenstein of Amherst College, in his recent wonderful *Quantum Strangeness*, reinforces the idea. He tells us that his long study of the quantum world has led to this: "We must understand that the world is utterly connected . . . The fall of a tree in Chile might be linked with a plume of dust on Mars. The fall of a sparrow in Norway might be linked with the birth of a baby next door." Beautiful, right?

And on YouTube you can find an exciting young physicist doing a TED talk called "Quantum Physics for 7 Year Olds." In this talk, Dominic Walliman tells us about something called quantum tunneling, in which a particle can *go through* a kind of wall and *appear* on the other side. Just like that. Isn't this amazing? And no, it isn't magic. It's science. And it's all around us, and it's in us, and so maybe we should be paying attention. Just like we can't see spirits and the soul, we can't see these little particle things, either. But they're there. Actually, they're us.

So now I have to wonder: does the soul reside in this quantum world? Is that where we can find it? Or maybe is there another "world" even deeper than that one?

In this regard, connecting two major dots, from American psychic and prophet Edgar Cayce to now, is Ervin László, two-time Nobel Peace Prize nominee and his book, *Science and the Akashic Field (An Integral Theory of Everything)*. I just love scientists who have such courage as to write a thing like this! (More about Cayce to come, in his own chapter.)

David Bohm

Well, I don't pretend to understand the science in the film I just watched on YouTube, but the work is amazing. I think anybody who loves physics will probably go crazy for it! The film is called *Infinite Potential: The Life and Ideas of David Bohm*. Bohm was called by Einstein his "spiritual son," while the Dalai Lama called him the "science guru . . . who opens our minds." The man was a living bridge between two worlds, and these giants recognized it. (His father wanted him to take over an electronics store, but this genius had bigger fish to fry, thank goodness!)

The Bohm film ends with these words from this amazing quantum physicist who worked at the "intersection of science and spirituality." He said, "The essential quality of the infinite is its subtlety, its intangibility. This quality is conveyed in the word, spirit . . . That which is truly alive is the energy of spirit, and this is never born and never dies."

Einstein and Spirit

Going now in a slightly different direction:

In 2002, a book of letters was published by Alice Calaprice. The book is called *Dear Professor Einstein: Albert Einstein's Letters to and from Children*. Calaprice is the author of many books on Einstein, she lectures on him around the world; and she's spent over three decades doing research on this man. In the *Letters* book, we find this excerpt from Einstein to a sixth grader named Phyllis Wright: "But also, everyone who is seriously involved in the pursuit of science becomes convinced *that some spirit is manifest in the laws of the universe, one that is vastly superior to that of man.* In this way the pursuit of science leads to a religious feeling of a special sort, which is surely quite different from the religiosity of someone more naive."

So, one of the greatest scientists of our time came to the conclusion, *through his work*, that there is a master spirit at work in the universe? Well, he did *prove*, using math and physics, that matter can't be destroyed. And what exactly is matter? Well, as I said, for one thing, *we* are matter. *We* are atoms and molecules and protons and electrons and neutrons and photons. *We* are made up of all kinds of invisible particles that can be weighed and measured. So think about it: if we are matter, and if matter can't be destroyed, which means *we* can't be destroyed either, then what is death?

And one more "little" thing: Einstein tells us that matter and energy are the same. It's just that one you can see, and one you can't. What does this mean? Well, it means that if the physical part of us dies (matter), *then we have to become energy.* And if you can't kill energy, then nobody dies. Okay, I get it. This is kind of simplistic. But I think it nails the idea down. We can't die, because we can't be created or destroyed. So, okay, our *bodies* can be created and destroyed. *But the essential energy of us* can't. See? It always was and it always will be. *We* always have been and always will be. Christ talked about the way and "the light." Was *this* what he was talking about?

And so, it's real science (along with Dr. Carl Jung and his work with metaphysics) that brought me to where I am today. And I think it's brought me to talking here about spiritualism and mediums and manifestations of the spirit side of things, so maybe a lot more people can see that *this isn't magic.* It isn't superstition. And for sure it isn't the work of some "devil." Stop being afraid! Just stop.

Actually, if the dead and I can communicate in a coherent and understandable way about beautiful things (which we seem to be doing these days), it's more likely the work of a god.

Well, the one I believe in anyway.

* * *

Reporting in the January 29, 2009 issue of *National Geographic*, Ker Than tells us this amazing thing:

"A potentially 'immortal' jellyfish species that can age backward—the Benjamin Button of the deep—is silently invading the world's oceans, swarm by swarm, a recent study says. Like the Brad Pitt movie character, the immortal jellyfish transforms from an adult back into a baby, but with an added bonus: Unlike Benjamin Button, the jellyfish can do it over and over again—though apparently only as an emergency measure. About as wide as a human pinky nail when fully grown, the immortal jellyfish (scientific name: *Turritopsis dohrnii*) was discovered in the Mediterranean Sea in 1883. But its unique ability was not discovered until the 1990s."

Wow, a lowly jellyfish that can reproduce itself forwards and backwards in time? How wonderful! These little creatures are defying death every day?

And, by the way, for any of you who look down on the TV show, *Ancient Aliens*, as total you-know-what? Think again. Most of every hour is devoted to ancient architecture, or NASA engineering, or geology, or anthropology, or quantum physics, or the historical records of numerous cultures, including their "bibles," or ancient religions, or ancient spiritual practices, or genetics, or astrophysics, or robotics. And, sure, they say that a lot of things that can't really be explained (yet) are the result of the possible "interference" of extra terrestrial life on our planet. But this is *only* to try and explain what scientists today admit they *can't* explain. Yet. So, if you don't believe in ETs, it's no reason to throw this TV baby out with the bath water. I mean, in a million years, I'd never have been able to write about that little eternal jellyfish if *AA* hadn't talked about it first. Or about Kaku and his opinions on "strings." Or about being able to watch an electronic scan of Deepak Chopra's brain function while he's in deep meditation. As I said, this is a brilliant show nobody should be missing.

Russell Targ

Finally, I want to mention here the work and experiences of physicist Russell Targ. Among other things, Targ and his team worked successfully for the US government military and intelligence communities for two decades in the area of remote viewing.

In Targ's fabulous book, *Limitless Mind*, he tells us, "We now know that our timeless awareness has mobility independent of our physical body." He goes on to describe the experiments of British scholar F. W. H. Myers, who spent "a good part of his life investigating mediumistic evidence for survival of human personality after death of the body." Needless to say, he says that Myers found the evidence he was looking for, and he recorded his experiences in his own book, *Human Personality and Its Survival of Bodily Death*.

Now I just want to say, if science is leading us today to an awareness of and belief in the eternal spirit, who am I to argue?

Chapter Three

The Spiritual Around
the World

I've come to the conclusion that after-death is a *two-stage* process. A lot of people choose to come back, to be reincarnated, but maybe not all. Or maybe not all people choose to come back right away. This makes them available for communication with the living world. Between lives, we can talk to them. I think.

So, this chapter is about reincarnation.

Dr. Ian Stevenson

Dr. Ian Stevenson was for many years the Chair of the University of Virginia Neurology and Psychiatry Department and Carlson Professor of Psychiatry and Director of the Division of Perceptual Studies at the University of Virginia. At some point in his career, Stevenson realized that science just wasn't explaining in a satisfactory way what he was finding in terms of the thinking and personality of some of his patients.

Stevenson noticed at some point that the majority of his most interesting cases were outside the United States. For this reason, he started traveling extensively, looking for answers, doing research that would last nearly forty years and sometimes involve arduous travel to places like Burma, Turkey, India, Lebanon, and Brazil.

In *Old Souls*, Tom Shroder tells us that Stevenson eventually accumulated a library of some three thousand cases involving both near-death experience and reincarnation. It's also noted that Stevenson at some point realized that most of the reincarnation-report cases he was finding around the world involved children ages two to four years old. (This agrees with much of what I've seen and read in the past twenty years or so about kids' reported "memories" of former lives.)

We're told that at some point in the midst of this research, Dr. Stevenson founded the Parapsychology Department at the University of Virginia. I'm so grateful to him and to this school for daring to venture in such a new and untested ("unscientific") direction.

Dr. Stevenson devoted years to his research and published several books on the subject of kids' past-life memories, including one on how the idea of reincarnation and science don't contradict each other. His books, including *Reincarnation and Biology*, have been published in the United States and in London. Another of his books, *European Cases of the Reincarnation Type*, chronicles many whose detailed memories as children led others to a belief that those children had indeed lived before.

As for other books on his findings: Dr. Stevenson was a prolific writer who produced many books on the results of his research and on his theories about science, and about life after death, and about the two together. So if you want to learn more, the material is out there.

And if you want to read a tremendous account of Dr. Stevenson's last trips to India and to Beirut, *Old Souls* is fantastic. Author Shroder went with Dr. Stevenson on these last two research trips, so he's able to provide rich first-person detail. I couldn't put the book down.

Carol Bowman

In the summer of 2021, I came across a fascinating interview with Carol Bowman, therapist and counselor and a past-life researcher who has worked for decades along the lines of Dr. Stevenson in his work with children's memories. "Past Life Memories: An In-Depth Interview with Carol Bowman" can be found on YouTube. Ms. Bowman has also authored several books on the subject, notably *Children's Past Lives* and *Return from Heaven*. I expect that those of you interested in the subject of reincarnation will find a treasure trove of information in the interview and in her books.

India / Tibet: the Dalai Lama

Among the world's cultures, it's in India where we find reincarnation as a basic cultural and religious belief of many millions. This principle is key to at least four of India's major religions (Hinduism, Buddhism, Sikhism, and Jainism). As with the ancient Greeks Pythagoras, Socrates, and Plato before them, India's religious followers have long believed in the rebirth of the soul. (The Greeks called this the transmigration of the soul, or *metempsychosis*. Dr. Raymond Moody tells us that Plato discusses in several dialogues "how the soul which has been separated from its body may meet and converse with the departed spirits of others . . ." In fact, in his *Phaedo*, Plato presents four arguments in support of the idea of immortality.)

Beyond that, the idea of reincarnation is that the soul of a person returns to earth after the death of the body of that person, then takes up "residence" in a new person. Moody also tells us, "If reincarnation does occur, it seems likely that an interlude in some other realm would occur between the time of separation from the old body and the entry into the new one." (This is my own area of interest and what pushed me to write this book. If this interests you too, you might be interested in another of Moody's books, *Reunions: Visionary Encounters with Departed Loved Ones*.)

The Dalai Lama is maybe the best-known example of the Indian concept of reincarnation. Followers believe that a Dalai Lama can *choose the body* into which he will next be reincarnated. The current Dalai Lama, the fourteenth, Tenzin Gyatso, has said that it's possible the next Dalai Lama could be female and that the search for the next might take a long time. (It took four years of looking to find the current Dalai Lama, Mr. Gyatso.) He has also said that if he's reincarnated, it won't be in a country controlled by China. (The current Dalai Lama, like all before him, was born in Tibet, which is today under Chinese domination.)

Another significant point in all this is that the Dalai Lama is acknowledged to be the religious leader of millions of followers.

But he also has major *political* influence among them. The Chinese government noted this in 1995, when it reportedly caused the disappearance of the six-year-old who'd been chosen to be the next Panchen Lama. This title conferred on the missing child both a religious and a *political* leadership position in Tibet. And so it's suspected that the Government of China felt threatened by what it must have seen as another new potential subversive influence. The idea of a Dalai Lama may be about religion for us Americans, but for China it's an issue of power. For this reason, also, the Chinese government drove the current Dalai Lama into exile. (He's the one most of you probably recognize from the news.)

India: Shanti Devi

As a little girl in India, Shanti Devi (1926 - 1987) started talking about her husband and family—those from her *previous* life. This started at the age of four, with the child talking about a previous existence in tremendous detail. Her parents began to think maybe she wasn't living in fantasyland after all, especially by the age of nine when she was able to describe the medical procedures that had been used to try to save her previous life after giving birth.

The girl gained fame throughout India. The upshot of this was that she was able to bring India's then-leader, Mahatma Gandhi, and a committee of influential officials to the house where she'd lived with her "former husband." There she was able to identify the people from her former life by name. She was able to describe the favorite meal of one of the family members. And when she met the son who had lost her, his mother, in childbirth, she cried. When she was asked how she could recognize a person she hadn't seen since his birth in another lifetime, she told her questioners that her son was part of her soul, and that *the soul is easily able to know such a thing*.

In fact, Shanti Devi may be the single most researched and investigated case in the world involving reincarnation. (She was interviewed throughout her life by many investigators, who all came away believers.)

But she may not be the only case.

The United States: 1950s
Closer to home, where we don't much take to the idea of reincarnation, there is the extraordinary story of Bridey Murphy, a woman who has become just as famous in this country as Shanti Devi is in her own.

The woman who said she remembered being Bridey Murphy was born Virginia (Ginny) Tighe on April 27, 1925. To all accounts, she lived an ordinary life in Colorado. But that would change overnight when Tighe went to a friend's party in 1952 and met Pueblo business-man Morey Bernstein. This man was successful and respected for his work. He'd also been intensely interested for years in the practice of hypnosis.

At the party, it's said that he successfully "regressed" Ginny Tighe. And the *New York Times* tells us that the hypnosis sessions that fol-lowed, "which began as a lark after a party, were conducted in front of respected witnesses who were willing to vouch for the apparent authenticity of [her] regression."

And what surfaced during the six experiences during which Tighe was "regressed" by Bernstein? What she gave him were detailed descriptions of a life in Cork, Ireland. She recalled being a woman named Bridey Murphy. Her story was repeated in detail by reporter William Barker in a *Denver Post* series, and the material later appeared as a bestselling book by Bernstein, *The Search for Bridey Murphy*.

For me, the fascinating thing is that Tighe, American through-and-through, often lapsed while hypnotized into a sometimes-heavy Irish brogue when recounting her life in Cork. She gave her date of birth in that life as December 20, 1798. She talked about her [purported] husband by name. She described the geography of the area in detail and gave place names. Occasionally she'd stop to translate a Gaelic word into English.

In a 2002 article in *The American Journal of Clinical Hypnosis* titled "The Search for Bridey Murphy" by Melvin A. Gavitz, you can find this:

"In the first session, she told of making a trip to the Glens of Antrim and passing by the Loughs of Carlingford and Foyle, explaining that 'lough' meant 'lake' in Gaelic. She mentioned the full names of a number of friends, such as Mary Katherine and Kevin Moore of Belfast. During the third session, she noted such specifics as reading the local *Belfast News-Letter*; she said that she lived in The Meadows district of Cork; she said there was a women's apparel shop called Caden House; that her husband taught law at Queen's University; and that she liked to cook his favorite meal of boiled beef and onions. She spoke of Irish folklore and history, citing a famous warrior named Cuchulain, and she added that her mother had read to her such books as *The Sorrows of Deirdre* and *The Tales of Emer*. When pressed by Bernstein, she almost always added such additional details."

Still, because none of the details Ginny Tighe gave about Bridey Murphy have been supported to date by fact, and because there were people and stories in *Tighe's own* young life that could have accounted for her command of the specific details she gave (although not for the brogue), one society dedicated to hypnosis concluded that this case was one not so much of memory of another life as one of stored childhood memories from *this* one. We are told, though, that the publicity about this Bridey Murphy case boosted interest in hypnosis a tremendous amount, as well as public interest in the field of hypnotic regression. And maybe one day we'll be able to know if Ms. Tighe was truly remembering another life.

***

I'd like to tell you: in the early 1990s, I had such a hypnotic regression, done with a psychotherapist in Manhattan. At the time, there was no Internet and no Google to check things by, though I did have a recording. But since I had no *facts* to rely on, I didn't really form an opinion on what I said during that hour-and-a-half. (I mean, maybe it was fantasy, maybe it wasn't.)

But then the Internet came along, and about fifteen years ago I transcribed the recording the hypnotist had made and started checking. What I found is that a great deal of what I said either proves out or is supported by recent facts coming to light.

And so, I have to wonder. What the heck *was* that?? See, I suspect my experience was not in any way ordinary. Because I've asked others about their regression experiences, and they've basically told me they were nothing like mine was. I mean, I "went back" twenty three thousand years, I was in a Neanderthal cave, I was at the French Revolution . . .

But what I find most interesting in all this is that I went to the hypnotherapist hoping to go back to my childhood in *this* life, to see what memories I might have buried when I was a kid. And, well, that just didn't happen!

The United States: Today

I've come across a website that's fascinating. It's hosted by a psychotherapist, Carol Bowman, who's written books on the subject of reincarnation and who tells past-life stories. The site is: www.reincarnation forum.com, and I find that it contains quite a few letters from readers who've experienced what they feel are really strange events. They remember and recognize things they've never seen or known, at least in this life. Bowman's focus is the self-reported memories of young children. Maybe this site and the people active on the site can help one of you reach a solution to your own puzzle!

Speaking of kids' early childhood memories, I've also found a book that's thoroughly reviewed by *The Daily Mail* newspaper in the United Kingdom. The book is called *Return to Life* and was written by afterlife researcher Dr. Jim Tucker of the University of Virginia. (He is Bonner-Lowry Professor of Psychiatry and Neurobehavioral Sciences at UVA, where he's also Director of Perceptual Studies.) This book presents ten years of research into children's memories. I mean, *crazy-specific* kids' memories of events in the lives of the dead that have been confirmed by people who knew the deceased well. He says now that he's convinced of the reality of reincarnation and, like me, he's trying to find the *science* that can logically support and prove that reincarnation is possible. If you Google the name of the book and the name of the newspaper, you should arrive at the extensive review I found online.

Jim Tucker is an interesting man. Born and raised in North Carolina, he attended Southern Baptist Church services. But he began to move away from purely Christian beliefs and toward a lifelong interest in past life research thanks to the influence of two people. He admired Dr. Ian Stevenson for putting aside mainstream science and spending his life looking for the principles, *the science*, that would support the idea of past lives. And he tells David Miller of sfgate.com that his wife was interested in new ideas: "Chris, though not religious, was open to topics I had given little thought to, such as psychics, spirits, even past lives."

I love his book, *Return to Life*. I'm so glad I came across it!

But now here's a thing that really bothers me: Dr. Tucker is an *American*. His book was issued by an *American* publisher. He teaches at a respected *American* institution. And yet I can find only one respected *American* newspaper that has covered the man and his work. (Maybe others are out there, but they sure aren't popping up on my Internet searching.) Is there a cultural bias in this country when it comes to things that can't be proved by science? (Yet.) And, see, this is really a terrible thing. Because what our media is doing is cutting off our access to anything that doesn't agree with what most others around the world believe. So then we have to rely on possibly iffy websites that are *also* ridiculed by American society at large. As I said, just terrible! Do they think we can't be exposed to stuff and make up our own minds?

And along the same lines—about information that must be kept from the masses at all costs—maybe you remember learning about Galileo? This was a scholar teaching that the Earth revolved around the Sun. For his "heresy" he was tried by the Catholic Church, found guilty, then kept under house arrest for the rest of his life. *This* is the kind of bias I'm talking about. It took the Church *three hundred years* to admit the man was right. Can you imagine?

And then there was poor Father Bruno, who also didn't luck out too well. The *Encyclopaedia Britannica* tells us that Giordano Bruno was an astronomer, mathematician, and philosopher who was ordained a priest in 1572. For the unpardonable sin of refusing to deny his claim that there are solar systems out there besides ours, in

1600 he was tried and convicted by the Church and burned at the stake for this "heresy."

So I encourage you to buy *Return to Life*. Not as an act of protest (!), but because it strikes me as containing a great bunch of reports from a respected academic and researcher. (You can also read *The Daily Mail* review first, then decide for yourself.) And while you're at it, among Dr. Tucker's other noteworthy works is *Before: Children's Memories of Previous Lives*. It occurs to me that any family lucky enough to have a kid who *remembers* is a lucky family, indeed, and they might want to know as much about the phenomenon as they can. The information is out there. Stevenson and Tucker would be a great place to start.

In fact, I think if you go to a bookstore and start hunting for books on reincarnation in general, you'll find them. Not all by trustworthy authors, for sure, but maybe you can find some with credentials. See, if brave people do their homework and report what they've found, they deserve the opportunity for others to know about it and, yes, even to question it.

England

Rosemary Brown's book, *Unfinished Symphonies*, starts like this: "The first time I saw Franz Liszt I was about seven years old, and already accustomed to seeing the spirits of the so-called dead."

Thus begins an utterly fascinating memoir by a woman whose global notoriety as a "medium" came from her ability to complete the unfinished musical work of brilliant, deceased composers. Like Franz Liszt, Johannes Brahms, Johann Sebastian Bach, Sergei Rachmaninoff, Edvard Grieg, Claude Debussy, Frédéric Chopin, Robert Schumann, Ludwig van Beethoven, and Wolfgang Amadeus Mozart.

Brown tells us that the other composers started coming to see her when "brought" to her parlor by Liszt. She tells us in the memoir that she formed personal relationships with some of these composers when they came to dictate to her the work they'd never had a chance to finish while on Earth (and in some cases, to *start*). In all, this amounted to over four hundred pieces of music.

Brown explained that proving herself to skeptics was always a problem. If a composer shared some unknown fact about his life, there was no way to verify it. And if some fact *were* known, she'd be accused of looking it up. So it was damned if you do, damned if you don't.

Something great happened along the way, though. Philips Recording Company recorded an album of Brown's music, as dictated to her by the greats, and the BBC did a documentary on her work. These things led a serious researcher to take an interest. Professor Doctor W. H. C. Tenhaeff, a psychiatrist and director of the Institute of Parapsychology at the State University of Utrecht in Holland, asked if Brown would be willing to be tested by his team of experts. He was looking for a brain diagnosis that could explain how Brown did (compose) what she seemed to have done. She readily agreed.

Among other things, though, the experts weren't able to explain certain stuff. For example, how could Brown have known things about the composers that would've been of little interest to almost anybody? The color and thickness of a boy's hair when he'd been a piano student of Liszt? That boy being a distant relative of a scientist-questioner? Clearly, Brown wasn't reading minds, because in this case the questioner didn't even know the story himself until he checked with his family.

In the end, Tenhaeff's group never came up with any kind of definitive answer, psychobiological or otherwise, to explain Brown's purported amazing feat. But what I think is that Brown had known Liszt during his lifetime and therefore he knew he could trust her in *this* life of hers to do his work and get it right.

Unfinished Symphonies was published in 1971, in the United States, by William Morrow and Company. Rosemary Brown died in November 2001 at the age of eighty-five. With the exception of the time when she was taking her musical "dictation," this woman lived a totally ordinary life.

And, boy, do I wish somebody would take another look with modern scholarship at the music Brown claimed was dictated to her by the great composers. Maybe a phrase here, a phrase there, a motif here, a motif there, will ring bells for an authority these days?

Finally, I'm sorry I don't know how to get hold of that old Phillips recording. But at least Brown's work was able to persuade somebody at that company, and so they made "her" music available to the world.

Italy

The story is told of Alexandrina Samona, who died at the age of five in 1910 in Palermo, Sicily. The story goes that after her death the girl came to her grieving mother in a dream and told her that she'd be coming back.

It appears this may have been exactly what happened. The mother became pregnant, gave birth to twins, and named one of the babies Alexandrina, because there was an uncanny physical resemblance to the lost child.

But the similarities didn't stop at the amazing physical duplication (facial asymmetry, the *same* problem with the right ear, the *same* problem with the left eye). Both girls also hated cheese, both were left-handed; both were obsessed with neatness and with clean hands. And, like the first Alexandrina, the second was content to play alone and amuse herself.

Japan

There's a rather profound tradition of reincarnation in the folktales of this Asian country. Author Alan Greenhalgh has looked into the Japanese stories of reincarnation, including that of a boy named Katsugoro. The boy was born in 1910, in the Edo period, and died of illness as a child. The story goes that he was then born to another mother and had solid memories of his previous life and home. The story can be found in the book, *Reincarnation and Misfortune in Old and Modern Japan: An Investigation of Traditional Beliefs and Modern Thought.*

Germany

Frankly, I didn't expect to find much from the practical and pragmatic Germans on the subject of reincarnation (shame on me for my *own* bias!). But the book, *Children Who Have Lived Before* by Trutz Hardo, stands out as a compilation of kids' stories. It's subtitled: *Children from All Over the World Prove That They Have Lived Before*. The foreword is written by Dr. Elisabeth Kübler-Ross, and this is enough to tell me the book has credentials behind it. Dr. Kübler-Ross was known all over the world for her academic interest in the subject of death and dying, and she was the author of many books on the subjects. Which means I have to think that Hardo's book on the kids is the real deal. (It's now on my list of things to dig into.)

Ancient Egypt

In a March 2002 article titled "Division of the Self" in the *Journal of Near-Death Studies* (springer.com), researcher Peter Novak tells us about the ancient Egyptian belief that "each individual had two souls, a *ba* and a *ka*, which separated at death unless steps were taken to prevent this division." He says that "Egyptian descriptions of the *ba* and *ka* are strikingly similar to modern scientists' descriptions of the conscious and unconscious halves of the human psyche." In this ancient culture, as in others, it was believed that one of these two souls "would go on to reincarnate." Meanwhile, today we see that the ancient Egyptian royals were dispatched to their eternal glory with all the things anybody could want to enjoy a rich and happy afterlife.

And now, in this single departure from the other references in this book, I want to recommend here an amazing novel, *the book of two ways* by *New York Times* bestselling author Jodi Picoult. It's astonishing to me, but it seems that while I was busy writing this book marrying the ideas of quantum physics with concepts of the afterlife, Ms. Picoult was busy writing a striking love story that marries the ideas of quantum physics with concepts of the afterlife as they were recorded by the ancient Egyptians. It's a great read (and the only fiction reference you'll find here, in *The Afterlife Book*). And, look, even if you're not all that interested in love stories, you may be interested in all you can learn here about the spiritual and scientific themes the author weaves so well.

* * *

When I started out on this chapter, I didn't realize what an enormous subject reincarnation around the world could be. Now I see there's just not enough pages here to cover it all. What I decided to do is tell you a few of the stories that have piqued my own interest and curiosity. If you're really interested, you can know there's work out there by even more serious people. Work by people who are taking a serious interest in the serious subject of life after death. (Among these in the past have been Johann Wolfgang von Goethe, Benjamin Franklin, David Hume, Arthur Schopenhauer, Leo Tolstoy . . . just to name a few who took the subject quite seriously.)

It's my hope that something here will prompt you to explore too!

Chapter Four

The Sleeping Prophet:
Edgar Cayce

Around the world and for centuries there have been many prominent mystics. Nostradamus, Rasputin, and Helena Blavatsky are probably the most well-known today. But so far, there's been just one major American-born mystic. And before I take us into yesteryear to look into the "mediums" who were active back when, I want to take a second (and a chapter) to celebrate this one astonishing man:

Edgar Cayce, probably the best-known American clairvoyant (psychic) to date, was born on March 18, 1877, in a small Kentucky farm town. Over the span of his sixty-eight years, he became renowned as a man who could predict the future and "remember" the ancient past. When asked how he was doing this, he explained that he simply "read" "the Akashic record" and repeated what he saw there. He told his listeners that this is the record of everything ever said and done on this planet, and, for some reason unknown to him, he was able to access it and read it. (Imagine if you were the only computer user with a keyboard able to reach "the cloud" and read to others what you found there! Well, I imagine Cayce's mental "keyboard" for reaching the Akashic record was pretty much like that.) He also told people he had no idea what it meant, exactly, this reading of the Akashic record, and he said he had no idea *how* he was able to do what he was doing.

(And THIS is so cool: Many times, Cayce refers to the fact that all our thoughts and actions are recorded in the Akashic record via the "*skeins*" of time and space, which he says are the same. Well, when I saw that word, "skeins," all I could think of is *strings*! I wonder . . . And then I realized about this space-time thing: Somebody asks, how far is the store from here? And somebody answers, ten minutes. Distance = time!)

The Association for Research and Enlightenment (A.R.E.), an organization founded by his sons to promote Cayce's work, tells us that early in his life their father was able to speak with his deceased grandfather. This psychic communication lapsed into the background as the growing boy went to school and started making a life. Ultimately, when a man, he worked as a photographer, he went to church every Sunday—he was basically a scholar when it came to knowing and reciting the Bible. Above all, though, he was a humble man who used his gifts to help others in distress.

His family says that when it came to helping anybody, Cayce was most interested in helping children. They also tell us that this extraordinary man didn't care about making money or profiting from his ability in any material way. He didn't care about fame. Looking around us today, I can't even imagine that.

In the course of his lifetime, Cayce gave thousands of "readings," on many thousands of topics, for thousands of believers who came to him for help. These subjects ranged from life on the lost continent of Atlantis to the building of the Pyramids to climate change. And he made untold numbers of accurate medical diagnoses for doctors who were stumped. (Cayce could even go in his mind to a drug store a hundred miles away, locate there a dusty bottle of medicine at the back of a back shelf, name and prescribe the use of that medicine for the person consulting him . . . and it would turn out to be the right thing at the right time in the right place. Who can *do* that!)

Even more interesting: his work has been accumulated, recorded and codified, and nobody has ever noticed any kind of contradiction between something he said twenty years before and something he said "yesterday." They say that people who tell lies eventually make a mistake. The liars forget what they said because they made it up on the spot in the first place. This is just one of the reasons Cayce was eventually believed by a lot of people. He never seemed to "make a mistake."

If you'd like to know more about Edgar Cayce and his gift, an enormous amount of material has been written by him and about him. Still, even with a lot of posthumous fame, the man seems to be regarded today as more a minor cult figure than a major presence in the world of spirituality.

Well, as far as I'm concerned, this isn't too great. It says a lot about our modern values, our American values. That a man with no other agenda than to help people however he could, and who did so with crazy-phenomenal success . . . that such a man can be so ignored as he pretty much is right now by mainstream society doesn't speak well of us. In fact, I'll bet that many of you reading this have never even stumbled across his name. And yet, "the sleeping prophet" (so named by a reporter who noted that Cayce always did his work in some kind of deep trance and on awakening never remembered what he said) . . . well, over the years, this 'prophet' produced so much work that Nostradamus' output doesn't even come close. (Then again, Nostradamus seemed to have a habit of predicting enormous calamities, and this is the kind of juicy stuff TV and movies are drawn to . . .)

Among the subjects Cayce addressed either directly or as context in readings when addressing other subjects were: astrology, dreams, ancient mysteries (like what Jesus was doing during the "missing years" of his life), modern mysteries like crop circles and the Dead Sea Scrolls, holistic health, life's purpose and challenges, meditation, oneness, spiritual growth, and reincarnation.

W. H. Church, in his book, *Edgar Cayce's Story of the Soul*, tells us that Cayce's readings describe life as cyclical: *from heaven to earth and back again*, and he said that between lives there is rest. (I believe this resting state is when souls are able to communicate with the living.) According to the very religious Cayce, in this evolutionary cycle of the soul, life begins and ends in the Mind of God. We come "down" for an ego experience; we go "back up" to gather the lessons we've learned here. (Kind of sounds like Einstein all of a sudden, doesn't it?) Jeffrey Furst's brilliant book, *Edgar Cayce's Story of Jesus*, gives us hundreds of excerpts of Cayce readings. One is this: "Also, during the interims between such (material) sojourns [earthly lives] there are consciousness or awareness. For the soul is eternal and it lives on—and it has a consciousness and awareness of that which it has built." Yes. Intelligence does persist beyond the grave, and yet another authority says so. Einstein, Cayce, and the ancient Greeks all say so. And yet we don't pay attention!

In another Cayce reading having to do with Jesus and the Apostles, they say he told his listeners about a "place" called "the Interbetween," where souls go between incarnations. He mentioned in this context the idea that Jesus and the Apostles had "*pre*planned" His life on Earth. (If this idea is correct, it would go a long way to supporting my idea that a great artist and I agreed long ago to "meet" in this lifetime of mine because we have work to do. But more on this later.)

Yes, I know that the idea of Jesus having many earthly lives is anathema to many, but this is what Cayce saw over many decades. In fact, in one reading he tells us: "The study from the human standpoint of subconscious, subliminal, psychic soul forces is and should be the great study for the human family . . ." and this from a churchgoing, god-fearing, Christian Sunday school teacher!

Look at it this way: historian Elaine Pagels tells us in *Beyond Belief* about the origins of what we've come to know as the New Testament. These are words Cayce would have known well. She tells us that it was basically *one man* who decided (for what to me seem to have been political reasons) to select the four Gospels we know today and to trash everything else.

The problem is that this trashed stuff sometimes contradicts in big ways much of what we've taken for granted for centuries. Look for the Gnostic Gospels and the Gospel of Thomas, for example. There are some fine books out there now on these subjects, about the documents found in 1945 at Nag Hammadi in Upper Egypt, about the better-known Dead Sea Scrolls.

All of this has led me to keep my mind open: Cayce was a *religious*, God-fearing man who told the world what he saw while he slept. If he saw that Jesus had been Adam (which he did), how are we to know this is false? The writer Church says at one point, referring to Cayce readings, " . . . we discover the Lord playing out the divine role as Wayshower through some thirty different incarnations in the flesh."

Church also tells us a story related by David Feldman, a Tufts University psychologist, about a ten-month-old boy named Adam. Adam asked his parents one day: "Please teach me logarithms. I understand the characteristics, but I don't understand the mantissa . . ." Needless to say, his parents were beyond startled. I say this was a memory that came with the boy from one of his previous lifetimes.

Church also reminds us of the thinking of 18th-century mystic Emanuel Swedenborg, who believed: ". . . there is a plurality of worlds" and "the human race is not from Earth only." This thinking is explored at length in *Compendium of the Theological and Spiritual Writings of Emanuel Swedenborg.*

So many great thinkers and philosophers over the years pushing us to broaden our horizons and take our blinders off! Or at least to suspend our disbelief long enough to allow different ideas to come in!

What is the bottom line? Cayce was telling us nearly a hundred years ago that we do not die. He was telling us that our physical form may disappear from the face of the earth. But the *energy* we are, the energy that comprises that form . . . that energy lives on. (Just as Einstein's science tells us.)

Cayce was really the pioneer in America who told his countrymen that, yes, we die, but only to be born again in *physical* bodies, to live new lives, different lives. (We're also told by other philosophers that any unfinished business in one life will crop up again and again in other, future, lives . . . until we get it right. Well, there's an incentive! I sure as heck don't want to have to repeat some of my more stellar mistakes even one time, never mind many.)

Basically, then, I'm saying it was Cayce who inadvertently took the juicy Victorian idea of séance and spirit communication a step further and higher. Cayce put the idea of communicating with the dead on a much more elevated and serious plane. It's ironic when you think about it. This mystic communicated with the dead by talking with the *living beings they had become next,* the people who were seeking him out for help in their modern (current) lifetimes.

Today, we have mediums, real ones—real, talented ones—who can relay messages from the deceased to *their* loved ones left behind. I'm glad to say, some of these folks have even made it to mainstream television. Maybe America is finally getting its spiritual act together? At least are we finally dipping our national toe in the water?

But look. I couldn't possibly succeed if I tried to give you here a full and complete history of the life and thinking and work of this incredible man, Edgar Cayce. If you want to know about the work that lives on in his name, you can look to the A.R.E., in Virginia Beach, Virginia. You can look at the shelves of major bookstores and (I hope) find at least a few of the many, many books that have been published to communicate his prophecies and his gift to the masses. You can search online. You can go to used bookstores and maybe get lucky. (Even here in Manhattan, though, his books aren't easy to find. So maybe the A.R.E. will end up being your best bet as a source for Cayce's work.)

Frankly, here's the thing. If you really want to know what this man said and how and why, you'll find a way. And then it will be bye-bye to the kind of misinformation out there that led a lifelong friend of mine to remark, "They said he was a charlatan."

Not.

Like that old medicine bottle, he's out there still—he's just been hidden at the back of some store somewhere, on a top shelf. And I'm hoping that talking about Edgar Cayce here in a book about life after death might lead a lot of people to reach up to that shelf, dust him off, and take a good new look at "the sleeping prophet."

In early times, a good man like this, so accurate and so seemingly connected to what lives above kings? Well, he might just have been burned at the stake once as a magician of the dark arts.

Thank God those times are gone.

Chapter Five

When We Reach Out: Mediums Back When

I've been using the word a lot. Time for a definition.

When it comes to spirit communication, what is a *medium*? A medium is a person able to communicate with the unseen world, usually on behalf of other people. These others are the believers who come to a medium to get answers to questions they can't get answered in ordinary ways. In today's language, mediums speak to the dead on behalf of the living, and the dead speak back in a "language" ordinary people may not recognize. But a true medium can.

Webster's defines *medium* as: "an individual held to be a channel of communication between the earthly world and the world of spirits." Sounds a bit like a *human* "string," doesn't it?

Anyway, throughout the course of history, those I believe to be true mediums all ply their trade in an honest way, while phony "mediums" (like phony "psychics") take the trust and the money of gullible people and give nothing real in return.

I think one of the problems we face here is that it's hard to tell the real from the bogus sometimes. How could observers possibly know? What tests could be applied? Today, we have the Internet at our fingertips. There's Snopes, the site that identifies frauds and scams. There's Wikipedia for at least basic information on people. Well, they didn't have any frames of reference like these in the mid-to-late 1800s to the early-to-mid 1900s. People had only their eyes and ears to trust. So, then, how many skeptics would it take to catch somebody levitating a table by pulling strings in the ceiling? How could somebody prove a photograph had been faked to depict spirits among the living? You can be sure, the fraudsters have always known how to thwart investigation. And they've always taken great advantage of the general ignorance.

Then there's the psychological problem (that persists to this day). How many people even wanted to *try* to catch the phonies? The fact is that most of us might not even *want* to tell the fake from the real. I know from my own work with thousands of folks that a great many of us really don't *want* to stop believing in what we can't prove or see. As you can imagine, among the population this kind of denial might be multiplied a thousand-fold when it comes to believing in somebody who claims to be able to deal with the dead on a regular basis.

I mean, the very idea of being able to communicate with somebody we thought we'd lost forever? Then it would mean that nobody actually dies, right? And as I said, we all *want* so badly to believe . . .

Among the believer group in the mid-1800s was scholar William James. While his brother, Henry, was busy writing romance novels, William was busy gathering together a group of like-minded people to explore the spirit world. Wow, romance and ghosts. Must have been quite some dinner table conversation in the James household!

They say it all started for James when he heard about a little girl named Bertha Huse. The child had disappeared off a bridge one icy New Hampshire winter morning. Searchers and divers could find nothing. But three days later, a woman downriver named Nellie Titus had a dream. When she woke up, she was sure she knew exactly where in the river Bertha was and in what condition her body would be found. A diver went to the spot, and there was Bertha, her body arranged exactly as Nellie had seen.

But things didn't stop with Nellie Titus. Things actually started with Nellie, the woman who got William James thinking serious thoughts about the supernatural.

In her book, *Ghost Hunters*, Deborah Blum reports that at the time " . . . James was a heralded professor at Harvard University, the author of the most respected text on psychology yet published, and a founder of the American Psychological Association. Yes, he had a lot to lose. But he said what he thought anyway: 'My own view of the Titus case consequently,' he said, 'is that it is a decidedly solid document in favor of the admission of a supernormal faculty of seership.'"

And, like Swedenborg, James believed that spirits and the living are tied together by invisible connections. (Here come those "strings" again!)

In fact, in a lecture he gave at both Yale and Brown universities, James challenged the idea that the world "should be understood only by the application of logic and science." To him, science has its limits. (This was the case, as well, for Albert Einstein, who is quoted as saying: "Condemnation without investigation is the height of ignorance." Amen to that.)

James also wrote in 1907 "A Case for Clairvoyance," an article in the *Proceedings of the American Society for Psychical Research*. I have to give the man credit. Like Dr. Carl Jung, who would risk the ridicule of his colleagues to explore the same uncharted, unscientific worlds, James had the guts to go for it. Even better, because he was so respected, he was able to gather together a group of eminent scholars willing to explore the spirit world with him.

Included below are some (but not all) of the cases of mediumship James and his group looked into. Despite the pitfalls of making any kind of list, I do want to give you here at least a smattering of the information out there on the mediums of old. I've chosen these practitioners because they acquired serious reputations at the time they worked. And if you want to know about the others I've left out, well you know what to do. (And if the information isn't online, I hope you'll be able to find it in a library.)

What I've tried to do here is talk about historical people whose names you might recognize and kind of tap dance in chronological order through the esoteric history of mediumship.

Helena Blavatsky
Madame Blavatsky is known as an occultist who cofounded the Theosophical Movement in 1875, in America. (The Society would be headquartered in India.) Her followers grew in number over time, and the Theosophical Society continues to this day. Among Blavatsky's early creative followers were artists Piet Mondrian and Wassily Kandinsky. American scientist and inventor Thomas Edison was also a Theosophist.

Theosophy teaches that freeing the spirit is the ultimate goal of our presence here on Earth, and that reincarnation is the process that the soul undergoes in its journey to that goal. Theosophy is founded in the ideas of brotherhood and the betterment of society through the betterment of the individual. It is not a religion. It is a philosophy that rests in part on the laws of karma. According to the organization's website, "The Human Soul is a pilgrim in a plan of Spiritual Evolution." (I love that!) *The Theosophist*, a journal, made its debut in the late 1800s.

Like Cayce, Blavatsky said she was able to read the Akashic record, although she called it "astral light," the universal memory. She taught that the essential nature of matter is energy, and she was doing this long before the quantum physicists arrived on the stage of science. She believed that physicality is an illusion. She taught that Theosophy is the true spiritualism, that Eastern spiritualism is the true philosophy and not Western mediumistic beliefs and practices. (This belief system made her a lot of enemies in the American mediumistic camp!) Her major work, *The Secret Doctrine*, brings together the old and the new philosophies as she attempted to act as a human bridge between them.

There's a wonderful 2013 docudrama on Blavatsky on YouTube, well worth watching.

Emanuel Swedenborg
Emanuel Swedenborg, who lived from 1688 to 1772, worked and researched in the worlds of physics, earth sciences, anatomy, and theology. He's also said to have spent about ten years investigating the

world of the spirits after an experience involving that world. In addition to this work, Swedenborg is known today for his psychic predictions and his efforts to understand hidden meanings in the Bible, not to mention his fame to this day for the church he inspired.

It's also possible that people only started taking him really seriously when Swedenborg died, since that happened on the exact day he'd predicted six months before.

Emma Hardinge Britten

Emma Britten, a pioneer in the British spiritualist movement and one of the founding members of the Theosophical Society, lived from 1823 to 1899. She demonstrated her psychic talents in the United States and is well known in some circles for giving the *Great Funeral Oration on Abraham Lincoln*, at Cooper Union, New York, two days after his assassination. (I've just read the *Oration*, and I can tell you it's a beautiful piece of writing—poetic, strong, politically insightful. I found this there: "Mourn for Abraham Lincoln with your hearts, but prove your love to him by taking up the burden he's laid down and finishing the noble purpose of his great life so untimely quenched." Well, that's just beautiful . . .)

As an adult, Britten worked as a trance medium. Her gifts had surfaced when she was just a child, when she was having visions that enabled her to predict the futures of the people she met. She was also able to give people accurate information about their deceased loved ones. As an adult, she was a clairvoyant who became active in a "secret society" that experimented with magnetics.

In an ironic twist, this mystic came from England to New York City to attend séances with the idea in mind of exposing them as hoaxes. Instead, she found herself hearing true information about her own life, from childhood on, and this occult experience is what led her to become an important part of the spiritualist movement. She's credited with writing and/or editing several books dedicated to the philosophy of spiritualism. In 1878 and 1879, she and her husband worked as spiritualist missionaries in Australia and New Zealand.

She died in 1879 at the age of seventy-six.

Daniel Dunglas Home

This medium was a Scottish mystic who worked in the mid-1800s. He's reported to have said he was here on Earth "on a mission." to demonstrate that we can live forever. We're told he refused to take money for his work, but I have to wonder about this. Because I've also read that while he didn't charge a fee, he did accept gifts.

Over his lifetime, Home's mediumistic abilities were demonstrated for a lot of people of high rank. It's said that even Sir William Crookes, chemist and physicist (and atomic theory pioneer) attested to Home's skill. In his *Quarterly Journal of Science*, Crookes stated conclusively his conviction that "psychic phenomena are real."

Home was brought as a baby from Scotland to Connecticut by an aunt and uncle after his mother found she just couldn't handle him. From his infancy, "things" had been happening around the boy (a cradle rocking by itself when he was in it, for example). Then maybe things went quiet for a while?

But when Home was a teenager, his world seems to have heated up again. Events started happening in the house that many today would attribute to poltergeists: strange rapping sounds, furniture moving around all by itself, things like that. History also tells us that these things only happened when Home was present, so, like his mother before them, his aunt and uncle threw him out. (Imagine! A teen on the streets . . .)

Yes, it's a bad thing to be just a kid and thrown out of one's house. But it also sounds to me like the couple set him free in a way, because it's reported that once on his own, Home started holding séances that people said weren't like any others taking place at the time. For once, this was a medium who was doing his work in daylight or at night in brightly lighted rooms. This was a medium who was making sure to have a number of men at the séance, to nab him if he tried to play games and fool his audiences.

But Home wasn't playing games. People felt that he was truly contacting the deceased. And so his fame in New England society was cemented.

In 1854, Home was diagnosed with tuberculosis and went back to Europe to live in London in a hotel owned by one of his followers.

There he achieved a following at the highest levels of European society. He conducted séances for Napoleon III and Queen Sophia of the Netherlands, among others. And his followers included novelists William Thackeray, Leo Tolstoy, Anthony Trollope, and Alexandre Dumas, as well as poet Elizabeth Barrett Browning. (I've read that Browning's interest in spiritualism created serious problems in her marriage. Husband Robert thought it was all a crock and had no use for Home.)

After holding more than fifteen hundred séances in two countries, Home fell for the last time to the disease that had plagued him for years. Tuberculosis finally caught up with him in 1886, when he died at the age of fifty-three.

(I add here, at the request of a Home fan: the man is reputed to have levitated, even as high as the ceiling sometimes, in full view of people, while in the midst of his communication with the dead. But being a practical journalist with a doubting mind, I think I have to put this feat in the same doubtful category in which President Lincoln rides a floating piano. *Maybe* Home could levitate. Then again . . .)

The Bangs Sisters
I want to mention here that I've found a lot of siblings in the history of spiritualism. These pairs worked together, although not necessarily demonstrating the same gifts.

One such sibling pair, Elizabeth (Lizzie) and Mary (May) Bangs, may be best known for a phenomenon unique to them that's called "precipitated paintings."

In the presence of the loved ones, the sisters would hold a piece of blank canvas in plain sight, and usually in about forty minutes a true likeness of the deceased would appear on the canvas.

Lizzie Bangs was born in 1859 and May in 1862. We're told that the sisters began to exhibit mediumship at the respective ages of eleven and eight. Before the paintings started to manifest, they were involved in many kinds of demonstrations that included automatic writing, clairaudience, and clairvoyance.

It's stunning to see (because you can) a couple of the portraits that were supposedly created by nothing but the mediumship of the Bangs sisters. N. Riley Heagerty has assembled twenty of the paintings in his *Portraits from Beyond*. And for an online preview, you can find a couple of these images at whitecrowbooks.com. You can also find some of the sisters' original paintings on display in the museum at Lily Dale, New York. (This phenomenon may be related somehow to what has been happening to me for six years, to be covered in detail later. If so, it comes closest to my own experience so far.)

May Bangs died in 1917, Lizzie in 1920.

The "Spiritual Knockers from Rochester"

So-nicknamed by a scoffing editorial in the *Scientific American* of the day, the website smithsonian.com tells us the Fox Sisters were brought to New York by believer Andrew Jackson Davis, himself a reputed seer. In 1847, Davis recorded (in *The Principles of Nature, Her Divine Revelations, and a Voice to Mankind*) what he claimed to be the content of messages given to him, in trance, by Emanuel Swedenborg. (Davis would come to be known in some circles as the "John the Baptist of Modern Spiritualism.")

So, when Davis heard about the Fox sisters purportedly channeling the spirit of a dead peddler in their bedroom in Rochester, New York, he invited them to his home in New York to see for himself. He liked what he saw, so they must've been doing something right.

The sisters (Maggie, Kate, and Leah) then embarked on a tour to "spread the word of the spirits." Among the converted who became major supporters of the two women were Horace Greeley (then the editor of the *New York Tribune*, who told the mediums they should be charging $5.00 per person for séances, and not $1.00). Others were *The Deerslayer* novelist James Fenimore Cooper, poet William Cullen Bryant, and abolitionist William Lloyd Garrison.

As time went on, though, particularly during the Gilded Age, the demand for what we'd think of today as miracles (I would, anyway) was exhausting the sisters. Then arguments broke out among them about betraying the principles of spiritualism, the *religion*, to the degree that one of the sisters ended up betraying them all by making a major speech in which she said the Fox's act was just that, an act, a sham. (She recanted a year later.)

And spiritualism was dealt yet another major blow when a second sister also started attacking it.

Meanwhile, each of the sisters was telling the world about various phony aspects of their "magic" act. The noises of the dead, for example, they said were really being made by them "clicking" their joints. And all this while the poor third sister was reportedly steadily drinking herself to death.

Despite all this self-induced negativity, though, there were some who felt that Maggie was a legitimate medium. These folks also felt that the three sisters basically lost their following because they fell victim to the anti-*religious* fervor of the day.

We're also told that, after all this, the Fox sisters never reconciled.

As an epilog to this story, per smithsonian.com: "In 1904, school-children playing in the sisters' childhood home in Hydesville—known locally as 'the spook house'—discovered the majority of a skeleton between the earth and crumbling cedar walls. A doctor was consulted, and he estimated that the bones were about fifty years old, giving some support to the sisters' tale of spiritual messages.

"But not everybody was convinced. The *New York Times* reported that the bones created 'a stir amusingly disproportioned [sic] to any necessary significance of the discovery' and suggested that the sisters had merely been clever enough, even as children, to exploit a local mystery. And even if the bones were that of the murdered peddler, the *Times* concluded, 'there will still remain that dreadful confession about the clicking joints, which reduces the whole case to a farce.'"

If you'd like to know more about the Fox sisters, I can refer you to the incredibly well-researched book by Barbara Weisberg: *Talking to the Dead: Kate and Maggie Fox and the Rise of Spiritualism.*

Were the three Fox sisters frauds? Did any have occult talent? Well of course I'm not sure, but I tend to think they were bogus. I just can't believe that mediums, who take their work really seriously and tend to attribute their abilities to a divine power . . . I can't believe that such people would lie about their gifts, never mind attack each other as viciously as the Foxes did. It seems to me that a true connection with things not of this world would tend to make somebody think twice about it, you know? (Then again, maybe I'm just too naive?)

Anyway, the Foxes started working at paranormal things in 1848, and, despite all their proved fakery, the start of spiritualism in America is nevertheless attributed to them.

Leonora Piper, "White Crow"

Harvard Medical School-educated William James (1842–1910), philosopher and psychologist, was a founding member of the American Society for Psychical Research and a member of its Committee on Mediumistic Phenomena. For more than two decades, as part of his research, James attended séances and sessions with mediums, trying to verify the existence of spirits.

As we're about to see, James's last wish may have been granted:

In his article, "The Medium Had the Message," published in the February 1971 issue of *American Heritage* magazine, Robert Somerlott tells us: "Mrs. Leonora Piper, the world's greatest psychic medium, was outwardly the world's most ordinary woman. . . . Socially and educationally, she is above the local mill women, but it would be too flattering to call her middleclass. The brown skirt and unadorned bonnet she wears give the impression of an underpaid schoolmarm. If we try to sum her up in a metaphor, she becomes a drab house sparrow slightly grayed by the factory smoke of Boston."

It was in 1884 that this reportedly very ordinary woman decided to consult a psychic healer in Boston to help her with a variety of ailments that had plagued her for years. She was bothered to the degree she had to carry practically a drugstore around with her everywhere she went.

At any rate, Piper's visit to the healer didn't help with her ailments. But she did find herself drawn to the kind of work he was doing. So she went back.

This second time at the healer, ". . . while seated with the other clients, Piper suddenly felt herself drawn into a state of suspended animation. The furniture appeared to whirl around her, her mind reeled, and collapsing on the table, she fell into a deep trance, apparently hypnotic. Her body convulsed, she groaned, mumbled, then began to speak—but not with her own voice."

History tells us that voice "belonged" to an Indian maiden (the idea of which is derided by the writer of the *American Heritage* article as prosaic).

But this moment wasn't to be the last of it. From this one experience, Mrs. Piper graduated to being able to put herself in the same trance. For the next four years, several "controls" arrived to take the place of the Indian girl.

Over time, we're told, the medium "was examined repeatedly by physicians, psychologists, and even vaudeville mesmerists, and their verdict was unanimous: Leonora Piper, as her conscious self, became utterly submerged."

For a while then, Mrs. Piper found herself dealing with people who believed in her without question. But that changed, when "In 1885 she became a subject for study by philosopher-psychologist William James of Harvard. Favorably impressed by his first findings, in 1887 James introduced Mrs. Piper to Dr. Richard Hodgson of the American Society for Psychical Research. From then until 1911, examination of Mrs. Piper was unceasing. Hired detectives often trailed her, volunteers watched her, her utterances were checked and double-checked, and every facet of her private life was scrutinized for evidence of fraud. No fraud was discovered. Mrs. Piper was integrity itself. After two years of intensive study, verification, and checking, Hodgson and James recommended that the British Society for Psychical Research invite the medium to England."

During the period of these investigations, until 1911 Piper conducted many séances in trance, and it seems she was right about everything. She was authentic; she was accurate, her readings were detailed. But over time, the work was beginning to wear heavy on her health. The last séance Piper held was in July 1911. She died in 1950, relatively obscure by that point.

Over the years, according to Piper, her "controls" included composer Johann Sebastian Bach, poet Henry Wadsworth Longfellow, and turn-of-the-19th-century billionaire Cornelius Vanderbilt.

I urge you all to check out the *American Heritage* article on Leonora Piper. It begins with this excerpt of an 1894 speech by Dr. William James, who became a total believer in this woman as a medium. James gave the speech on the occasion of becoming president of the Society for Psychical Research:

"If I may be allowed the language of the professional logic shop, a universal proposition can be made untrue by a particular instance. If you wish to upset the law that all crows are black, you must not seek to show that no crows are; it is enough if you prove one single crow to be white. My own white crow is Mrs. Piper. In the trances of this medium I cannot resist the conviction that knowledge appears which she has never gained by the ordinary waking use of her eyes and ears and wits."

Gladys Osborne Leonard
It all started for this trance medium when she was eight years old and learned of death for the first time when her father's friend passed on. This was the moment when she learned of the finiteness of life. This was the moment when she learned of burying people deep in the ground "so they can't get out." This was the moment when she learned of the terrible loss experienced by those left behind. This was the moment when she learned how people can just "disappear" overnight.

Leonard herself tells us in a manner of speaking that her child's mind was thrown into terror at the sheer enormity of all this, and she was tormented for many years afterward by the idea of death.

But something else was happening at this time, too. Gladys Leonard was becoming a psychic. Or, maybe, more accurately, her gifts were being encouraged to surface.

As she tells us in *My Life in Two Worlds* (the complete text is online):

Early every morning, sometimes before even being dressed or having her breakfast, she would see visions of beautiful places. No matter what she was looking at, the thing would disappear and instead there would be "valleys, gentle slopes, lovely trees and banks covered with flowers of every shape and hue." Her view seemed to go for miles, and she was aware that she was seeing farther than ordinary eyesight could take her. She tells us, "The most entrancing part to me was the restful, velvety green of the grass that covered the ground of the valley and the hills. Walking about, in couples usually and sometimes in groups, were people who looked radiantly happy. They were dressed in graceful flowing draperies, for the greater part, but every movement, gesture and expression suggested in an undefinable and yet positive way: a condition of deep happiness, a state of quiet ecstasy." These visions made her think how different those people were from those of us "Down here," because everybody she saw was "full of love and light and peace . . . No fear, or doubt, or dreadful mystery" was there. "It all looked too expressive of Life and Joy to be in any way connected with the unsatisfactory state in which I mentally lived."

But the kind of visions the child was experiencing were totally unsettling to her devout Christian family. Still, it seems that she persisted in telling the family all about them, in glorious Technicolor detail, until they finally forbade her to "see or look at her 'Happy Valley' again." (Imagine!)

I have to suppose this wasn't something Leonard could oblige them at. And who would *want* to? A child in terror of death comes upon such a *beautiful* place, and she doesn't even have to close her eyes to be there? (I'm guessing here that this is how she must've felt. Though she also tells us that the beautiful visions gradually disappeared.)

Then, according to Leonard, when she was a teenager, " . . . my Guides made several attempts at various times to draw my attention to Spiritualism, in the hope that I should be able to understand and use the psychic power that they knew I possessed."

And then one day she was drawn to a presentation by a medium. This woman selected Leonard out of a large audience and proceeded to tell her about the drowning death of her cousin, Charley. The medium also told the girl she had guides who were preparing her for the "special work" she was to do, as that medium herself was doing. Leonard tells us she was "walking on air" after this experience and again hurried home to tell her mother, to bring her mother the joy she herself had just experienced.

No such luck.

Once again, her mother commanded, "Stop!" in what Leonard says was a terrifying voice. "All you are telling me is vile and wicked, and I forbid you ever to go to that place again, or do anything further in the matter. It is dreadful. You will have some terrible thing happen to you if you follow such evil practices. They are evil, I tell you, evil."

And because Leonard had no support or encouragement for this new thing anywhere in her own ordinary life, she did basically stop going to the "vile" and "evil" places.

(It's ironic to me that, when her mother died, the medium says she saw a white light and knew it was her mother and checked the time. The visit had happened in the middle of the night. When she did get word of her mother's death, it was all as she'd seen it. Her mother had died at that time, on that night.)

From this point on, we learn that Leonard continually "bumped into" people who were spiritualists, people who were believers. And so she finally found the support and encouragement she needed, outside her family. (As I said, this "bumping into" people who believed as she did also happened to me, mostly in one short week, when I realize now that I was being launched as a professional psychic. The seed was being planted by a bunch of things that looked totally random . . . as it was meant to seem.)

As she grew, Leonard studied to be an actor and singer, but her voice wouldn't cooperate. And then one day, as she sat at a table at a séance, she says, " . . . a Communicator came who gave her name as 'Feda' and explained that she was an ancestress of mine. She had married my great-great-grandfather." 'Feda' told Leonard by spelling out words [with some kind of aid of the table] that "she had been watching over me since I was born, waiting for me to develop my psychic power so that she could put me into a trance and give messages through me."

From then on, thanks to the geography of London, every night Leonard was able to explore the world of mediums while working at a nearby West End theater.

From the *Encyclopaedia of Psychic Science* by Nandor Fodor, we learn: "In her autobiography Mrs. Leonard narrates many interesting out-of-body experiences. She often meets people in the spirit world and brings back memories of such meetings into the waking state. These spiritual excursions have often received striking confirmation through other means."

Gladys Leonard died in 1968 at the age of eighty-six.

Eusapia Palladino

There was a lot of controversy at the time about whether this woman could actually move furniture, levitate, manifest "spectral" hands, make trumpets blare, and in general accomplish feats of the physical mediumship that were throwing quite a few observers for the proverbial loop.

Eusapia Palladino was born in Bari, Italy, and orphaned by the age of twelve. She eventually found shelter with a family for whom she was supposed to work as a nursemaid, but, as with Dunglas Home, these people weren't happy about the strange, disconcerting things that started happening in their house after she got there.

At some point, Palladino started holding séances at which she was able to demonstrate what were said to be remarkable abilities. Eventually, researcher and investigator Cesare Lombroso sought out Palladino for some private séances. He wanted to evaluate her abilities (and evaluate of course the legitimacy of what she was doing). His published report says he found Palladino to be the real deal, and so several other serious investigations followed.

Over the years, Palladino was poked and prodded, so to speak, by academics from all over Europe. The investigators eventually concluded that Palladino wasn't averse to cheating. Then again, she *did* also manage to do some things that couldn't be explained.

Troy Taylor, in his review of Palladino for *The Haunted Museum* (an online publication), concludes this way: "Could Eusapia Palladino have been the 'real thing'? Was she truly a person who was able to harness that 'unknown force'? Or was she merely a clever hoaxer who managed to turn the tables on scores of observers who she saw as her intellectual and social betters? Did this common peasant woman have the last laugh?"

Well, I suppose we'll never know. But she's here in this book because others took her seriously enough to check her out and, also, well, because she's kind of famous for this stuff.

Estelle Roberts

This famous British medium was born in a London suburb in 1889. Although she claimed to have had encounters with spirits as a child,

Roberts didn't start working to develop her mediumship until she was in her thirties.

According to the website, InsightsFromSpirit, " . . . in the 1950's [Roberts] was greatly instrumental in the legal recognition of Spiritualism by the British government. Winston Churchill led the movement to remove the Witchcraft Act, which regarded the holding of séances as a criminal offence punishable by imprisonment. Estelle conducted a convincing demonstration of mediumship inside the House of Commons. She is regarded by Britain's spiritualists as one of its finest exponents of mediumship in the 20th Century." (I've looked for official recognition of this House of Commons claim, and so far I haven't found it. But it seems rather far-fetched for people to have simply invented the idea of a medium in the British lower House.)

At any rate, as with others before her and since, Roberts had both her doubters and her followers. Among the latter was ardent supporter Sir Arthur Conan Doyle, writer of the "Sherlock Holmes" crime stories. We're told that she " . . . filled the Royal Albert Hall in London on over a score of occasions, and she also toured the UK giving demonstrations of her exceptional mediumistic gifts to many thousands of people."

(By the way, there's a fascinating long entry on the website, Psychics Directory, by author Lilly Willis, titled, "The Psychic Side of Winston Churchill." Willis names Roberts here as Churchill's helper in achieving the repeal of the Witchcraft Act. But I have to say I can find no official statement connecting these two people.)

The Oracle at Delphi
Finally, I think I'd be wrong not to include here this ancient prototype. Because probably the best-known medium in Western culture is the ancient Greek Delphic Oracle. This "oracle" was actually a series of women chosen for the job of serving the people in the 8th century BCE. And, sure, we learn about this oracle in school, but I don't recall my own teachers going awfully deep into what these females were actually supposed to be *doing*. Yes, they tell us in school that the oracle spoke with Apollo. But then they kind of gloss over entirely what that *means*. A human having a chat with a *god*? Really? And a useful chat, at that?

As with the work of the traditional medium, the Delphic Oracle's job was to listen to people's questions and ask the god Apollo for answers. She would then tell the questioners what he'd said to her.

We know from historians that the work of this oracle could be done by any woman (age, class, education, level of wealth, marital status didn't matter), as long as she was found to be able to speak on behalf of the god. (Although there *is* a suspicion floating around that these women could do this only because they used hallucinogenic drugs before setting up shop for the day.)

Well, I suppose that's as good a suspicion as any for explaining what may never be explained. But it doesn't matter to me *how* these women managed to do their work. It only matters that so very long ago there was an acknowledged and respected living human who was *officially* designated to act as a communicator between the unseen world and man. There was a living human whose answers are said to have been so on target that they enabled government leaders to preserve the Greek state on more than one occasion.

This *official* thing is for me the whole enchilada, kind of a *Good Housekeeping* seal of approval on something most officials would think is bunk.

At any rate, the Oracle of Delphi is to my knowledge the first recognized medium to have had such an official stamp of approval from the powers that were.

* * *

A little aside here:

Do you know that the government of the United States was experimenting with parapsychology for decades and maybe still is? Do you know that the US Central Intelligence Agency was doing volunteer "remote viewing" exercises for a long time, with the idea in mind of military applications for psychic work, and that the US Defense Intelligence Agency was running the Star Gate Project for about twenty years, until 1995? (This was to investigate the potential applications of psychic work for espionage.)

And do you know that Russia (formerly the Soviet Union) was right in there, too, exploring psychic phenomena from a scientific point of view? I can recommend a fabulous book on some of the results of the Russian research, past and present: Sheila Ostrander and Lynn Schroeder's *Psychic Discoveries Behind the Iron Curtain*. Here we can find dowsing, "The Bulgarian Oracle" and her ability to "see" with her fingertips, Leonid Brezhnev ("healed by *psi*"), and a great many healers, scientists, researchers. The book is a trove of information too vast to list it all here.

As for an authority closer to home, physicist Russell Targ's book, *The Reality of ESP: A Physicist's Proof of Psychic Abilities*, is fabulous. Targ was instrumental in running the US government's remote viewing experiments at Stanford University. In this provocative book, Targ devotes a whole chapter to the persistence of "something" after death. He cites F. W. H. Myers's *Human Personality and the Survival of Bodily Death*. He also cites Stephen Braude's *Immortal Remains*, as well as Gary Doore's *What Survives?*

But this part to me is *the* very big deal: as at Delphi, there has been an *official, mainstream* stamp of approval by modern major world governments for at least spending a few dollars/rubles to look into things we don't really understand and maybe never will. And no, the US government claims it didn't grab the brass ring with the remote viewing and psychic experiments we now know about (which lasted two decades). But reports do tell us there were some successes.

* * *

Okay, that was a short list, I grant you. But I hesitate to mention here the people who are suspected of being out-and-out frauds. As it is, I'd be out on a limb to name any who haven't been suspected, since I've seen none of them at work. But I figure that a few anecdotes can't hurt. Right?

* * *

Another important note:

In 1951, Britain revoked The Witchcraft Act of 1735 and replaced it with The Fraudulent Mediums Act. If you read between the lines, this is a clear acknowledgement that somewhere out there among the frauds must be at least one true practitioner. Worthy of note here is that the well-known medium Helen Duncan was imprisoned for nine months under the old law.

Then, in 2008, a new European Union Consumer Protection Regulation was enacted to further protect the public from bogus "psychics." According to the Spiritual Workers Association website, ". . . the new law covers all spiritual workers, or spiritualistic service providers. This means you have to deliver exactly what you say."

I *love* that! First it tells me that in the mid-20th century the British government discovered that not all spiritualists are frauds . . . otherwise, why bother to institute a law specifically *against* frauds? And it tells me that today the European Union is going a step further in what I consider the right direction.

Back here in the United States, though, nobody has noticed yet that some psychics might actually be for real. And so, here there is no official recognition of the work of people like me. See, many of us do actually manage to "deliver" and help a lot of people, yet our government says we're "telling fortunes" for "entertainment" purposes. It would be my heart's desire if this country would just wake up as Britain has.

Look, bunko artists (ask the police) are *not* psychics. They're just crooks, plain and simple. And there are a lot of them out there, eager to separate gullible and innocent and desperate people from their money. As a matter of fact, Bob Nygaard, a retired NYPD detective, was making it his mission in life to bust every storefront "psychic" fraud he came across. (Thanks, Bob.)

But as long as our nation pooh-poohs *everything* and throws the baby out with the bath water, nothing is going to change for the better here in the United States. What we need are regulations that make sense. We need an informed society. We need open minds.

I go out on a credibility limb in this book because I'm hoping that a book like this can help pave the way to the acceptance we so need *and* to the correct legislation.

But I'm not holding my breath.

Chapter Six

When We Reach Out:
Mediums Today

This is from *The Telegraph* (London), June 24, 2018:

"Reincarnation is the in thing now, as spiritualism was after the First World War. It meets a longing for a life beyond the mundane. Spiritualism was not discredited by exposure of table-turning tricksters with Red Indian friends on the other side and false ectoplasm on this side. It just grew unfashionable, like the aspidistra.

"Now it's the 'spiritual' without the -ism. This takes in crystals, angels, standing stones, Gaia, a diet of fruit and nuts. Reincarnation, coherent or not, hardly deserves to be thrown into the same bran tub. Christians, though, believe, according to their creed, in almost the opposite, declaring that they look forward to the resurrection of the body. But that's another story."

Implied in all this reporting is a warning, really: be careful who you trust. Not everybody can do everything he/she claims.

In this regard, I want to say something: there's a bunch of famous mediums working today in the United States. Such is the power of television and the Internet that in almost any given week you can watch somebody in the comfort of your own living room talking to dead people at a kitchen table somewhere else. With one exception, my experience with those I talk about here has been limited to seeing them work on TV and from books they've written. But I like to think I have good radar for this stuff.

So here goes, *with this caveat*:

If I'm ever proved wrong about any of these folks, I won't know what to say . . . I just hope that all you newbies out there will keep an open mind but also a clear eye when it comes to evaluating the honesty of "seers" who say they can converse with the dead. I mean, this is a *gift*, people. (And I doubt it can be taught and learned unless somebody has the gift *already*.) And I hope you'll all realize that general statements that could apply to anybody aren't any proof of a darn thing. Somebody tells you, "Your grandmother cared a lot about you." So? Probably true for a *huge* percentage of people, right? Which means this kind of information is meaningless in the grand scheme of things.

What am I saying? I'm saying to keep an open mind, but at least listen for specific information that *only* the spirit in question could know. Just don't be wanting anything so much that you throw logic and common sense out the window . . . not to mention your hard-earned money. (Like they say, "Trust but verify.")

Probably the most important thing for me is ethics in professional practice. The idea of professional and personal ethics is one of the reasons you won't find a few other well-known TV mediums covered in this book. Either I just don't trust their motives, or I just can't put myself on the line for somebody I have no experience with. I mean, I haven't seen them work, I haven't heard their words, I haven't observed their body language while they work. Are they emotionally all-in when they do a reading? Do they seem to be guessing? Do they come across as *kind* people? No? Then just forget it! Life, especially the spiritual life, isn't supposed to be about money, right?

Now, look: You don't have to start doubting the people you have reason to believe in. But be careful. Just keep in mind that they work in an unregulated world.

In alphabetical order:

George Anderson

This was the first medium I ever saw at work. It was at least twenty-five years ago—this means he would've been a pioneer medium for our times. *The* pioneer, I should say. When I saw Anderson, he was on TV doing a group reading. There were maybe thirty people in the room. He would notice particular people and tell them who was there and what the spirits wanted them to know.

Although I hadn't put much faith in mysticism and the super-natural up to that point, I was impressed enough by Anderson to go out and get his first book on life after death. It's called *We Don't Die*. I read it pretty much in a day and continued to be impressed. I ended up feeling as if I could trust this man.

Today, I see that he's been working as a medium for over forty years and has been impressing a lot of other people all that time. And this includes scientists and skeptics. He lives on Long Island, New York, and I recommend his website.

(And, by the way, when young he was committed to a state hospital with a diagnosis of schizophrenia. Which he did not have. But that is how the world works: if you don't understand it, maybe it's just plain crazy.)

Theresa Caputo

The "Long Island Medium": yes, another medium from this finger of land that points out from New York City into the Atlantic Ocean. Caputo was kind of a fixture on TV for several years, and it's where I watched her a bit, at work with clients.

As I feel about George Anderson, something about this woman tells me she's the real deal. This is an ordinary housewife with a seeming extraordinary gift. She comes across as a cheeky woman, but what stands out most for me is her compassion. There's something in her that's just plain kind. (At least, that's what I *feel* when I watch her work.) She's also an author, and I love this: one of her books is called *You Can't Make This Stuff Up*. Well, I look at my own life and I can attest to that! And, look, I doubt very much *Shark Tank's* Barbara Corcoran (a "shark") would have let herself be filmed, speaking openly about her mom, in the midst of a reading by Theresa. At some point, I found tears coming from my eyes . . . I didn't know I was crying . . . but it was beautiful.

John Edward

This medium (yet *another* Long Island guy!) is maybe one of the best known in the United States today. For several years, he hosted *Crossing Over* on TV, and he and his books continue to be in circulation. I remember reading his first, *One Last Time*, and I remember being impressed. It's probably for the reason of his vast TV presence and popularity that Edward has been investigated and tested a lot by believers and scoffers alike. As far as I can tell, they've landed on both sides of the fence when it comes to his accuracy and skill as a medium. I have no position on this one way or another, but a dear friend attended a taping of *Crossing Over* long ago. She reported being "blown away" by what he was able to tell her. And since the man has been doing this work for thirty years, I have to believe he continued doing something right.

Matt Fraser

This young man I saw one time, on TV in June 2021, on YouTube. In the clip, he was explaining to a woman and her daughter how the son had died. This was the mother's only *unspoken* question, and he seemed to go right to it. Watching this, I felt this medium to be authentic, accurate, compassionate, and caring.

Eileen Garrett

Other than this Irish-born medium, I'm having a hard time coming up with any other prominent practitioner in the 20th century. I mean, the period after the 1920s and before the 1990s. I found Garrett only because I knew about Andrija Puharich and his Faraday Cage work (see the chapter on Devices), and she's mentioned in a write-up about him. So it looks as if, at least in the United States, not a lot was happening during that seventy years when it came to human-to-spirit connecting.

But I do find that Garrett was active in the 1940s. Among other things, in 1943 she published *Awareness*, which is a book dealing with her thoughts about psychic ability, consciousness and faith, basically. (This book was reissued in 2007 by the Parapsychology Foundation.)

As others were, Garrett was tested over the years. And the results were the same as elsewhere: Some found her psychic ability to be exceptional. Others said she was simply average. (So, what exactly is "average" psychic ability? Who devised an impossible rating scale? We're either psychic or we're not . . .)

I include Garrett in this book because, as I said, it seems there wasn't a lot of mediumship going on in America in the mid-20th century. And this woman stands out at least as a pioneer and a visionary.

If you'd like to know more about her, you can check out parapsychology.org.

Garrett died in 1970 in Nice, France, at the age of seventy-seven.

Wendy Newirth

A friend called today, and she happened to mention Wendy, "the psychic's psychic." Suddenly, I remembered this woman from her TV show long ago! I remember the accuracy of her comments, as confirmed by the people who were calling in. I remember the detail she was providing. I also remember so clearly Wendy's face, which I hadn't seen for decades until I looked her up online today. Today, I also discovered that Wendy works in Dobbs Ferry, New York, where I spent many happy weekends this past summer, and where I found my first book on sale in a little psychic shop there on Cedar Street. (Yes, it *is* a small world.)

Because I watched Wendy work on TV every week for a long time, and because I could see at the time how gifted she is, I'm including her here in this list.

Jeffrey Wands

I write about Jeffrey in *The Language of Tarot* because this is the medium I myself went to see on September 20, 2017. When I called for an appointment, his secretary gave me a couple of options, one of which had SO much significance I had to choose it. First, it happens to have been the birthday of my grandfather, the one who happened to be very interested in electricity and hypnosis. Second, it happens to have been the birthday of my older sister (who died shortly after arriving on the planet). Third, for you astrologers out there, the 20th happens to correspond to the exact degree of my ascendant (not an insignificant thing).

So, I did and I didn't plan this "perfect date" thing.

Clearly, there are no accidents! (Just ask Einstein . . .)

And how this came about in the *first* place?

Well, this is interesting: I'd been walking a dog for a lady in my building here in Manhattan. One day, after several years of helping her, for some reason I mentioned Jeffrey Wands and his book. She said, "Oh I saw him a few months ago."

I was kind of stunned. See, I'd been recommending him ever since his second book came out in 2007: *Another Door Opens*. It turns out he had predicted her twins long before she became pregnant. And it had never clicked with me that he was living and working so close to my home.

No, I'd never seen this man work, but I'd read that book, and I just knew he's okay. Why? Because he's very clear in this book about the idea that some people who come to him need *professional mental health help*. When he sees this, he refers them to psychotherapists, and he bows out of the picture. In fact, at the end of his book Jeffrey publishes extended comments by three therapists who know his work *and* his heart.

(I, too, have spent three decades sending folks to therapy. It would be a sin to pretend to be helping somebody and knowing at the same time that what they *really* need is professional help. Never mind knowing this and *still* taking their money. So, when I got to this section of the book, I was sold. It was that ethical thing that turned me on to this man in the first place.)

But ten years passed after that book came out. Ten years until this "random" woman told me she'd just had a session with him. And then I was suddenly totally psyched. I suppose it was just "time" for me to do this thing. Time to dip my own toe in the water and visit a medium. Time to hear what he—and maybe my loved ones—might have to say.

So then . . . destiny at work here, right? Oh, yeah.

Jeffrey Wands lives and works in Port Washington, New York, on the North Shore of Long Island. (Yes, Long Island. *Again*.) He and his wife have a modest yellow house on a modest tree-lined street maybe ten minutes on foot from the Long Island Railroad station. When we met, I discovered he's also just plain modest himself. Humble, even. It was a nice thing to discover.

Anyway, it was a warm and beautiful afternoon on the cusp of autumn 2017. When I arrived for my session, I was asked to wait in an outer room. It was there I had my first experience with this medium. As I sat there watching through the doorway, there was Jeffrey in the other room telling the cable guy to go home and reassure his mom. There was something personal going on about her own mother's passing. And just then I started smelling the trace odor of a hospice, followed by a slight floral scent. I looked around me. Nope. Nothing but a bamboo plant in there. (Was it the cable guy's grandmother I was sensing?) Then, just as fast as they came, the smells were gone.

To be honest, this hasn't happened often in my life, this thing with detectable odors floating past me from no source whatsoever. In my apartment I've smelled beer, the scent of lilacs, and the scent of other flowers. But it's happened only a few times maybe, and really, I've never been able to attach a loved one to a particular scent. Others tell me they've had the same experience. So I figure this aroma thing may be a lot more common than we know.

Anyway, maybe five minutes passes as I wait for my appointment, and then it's my turn. Jeffrey ushers me into a small office. I remember nothing about the room now except that it's furnished, and he has a computer system of some sort. Ordinarily, I notice details, but that day I had bigger fish to fry.

I'd barely managed to sit in the chair—apologizing if I was late, having been on the train—when the medium tells me that my father is saying, "It's a heck of a lot better than being stuck in traffic."

Which is *exactly* what my father *would've* said. Hunh. My traffic-hating dad.

But that was just the start. After this came forty-five minutes of confirmation of things I've experienced, seen, felt, known. Jeff gave me information about specific people and their specific quirks. (For example: I mentioned at some point that I didn't know until recently that my old Aunt Concorde read cards. Jeffrey said instantly, "Playing cards." So true.)

At any rate, my parents and the man I loved and lost were there. All acting as they did on Earth, really. My father was dominating the conversation, my mother was quiet as usual in the background. (Well, you better believe I gave her a talking-to after I left. I told her it was finally time to start using her damn *voice*. I do hope she was *listening*. But, yes, probably she did hear me, at least.)

See, Jeffrey was also able to confirm what I've felt for a long time: *talk out loud to those you've lost*. It makes them feel good to hear from you. Do NOT feel like an ass for doing it. These people are in your heart. They may as well be in your voice and your words, right? Talk to your deceased dogs and cats and birds and hamsters, too . . . tell them hello, tell them you love them. I mean, how can it hurt?

But the single most important thing that happened that day with Jeffrey Wands? I was seventy-two years old. I'd just embarked on a career as a writer (it's a long way from magazine journalism, where I was, to the world of books, where I want to be). Also, I'd developed a new interest in drawing.

But . . . *the age thing*.

So, I'd gone to Jeffrey that day with an *unspoken* question. It had been on my mind for a little while. Had I accomplished my mission here on Earth? Had I already helped all the people I was supposed to help? Had I already fought all the right battles and learned the right lessons? Was it about to be my time to move on? I hoped not.

Anyway, I suppose from this vantage point today, years later, that was really the *only* question I had. *Was I done on this Earth now?* Had I accomplished everything I was put here to do?

And all of a sudden, out of nowhere, the medium announces, "It's not over."

Imagine that.

On the train ride to my session, I just had the feeling it was to be the first day of the rest of a brand-new life. But I couldn't have imagined in a million years how much of a "first" it would be. And I couldn't have imagined that maybe I'd still be around for a next chapter. A big question *not* asked. But a big question answered.

See, *the upshot of that amazing forty-five minutes is this book.*

This medium also told me, among other things, that I would publish "many" books. And he said that the "others" in the room wanted the books to be on subjects like this one. (There was nothing specific, just that it wasn't supposed to be fiction.) And who am I to argue with a bunch of spirits who cared enough to show up for me that day?

And here we are now. Chapter Six and rolling right along.

Thanks, Jeffrey.

Lisa Williams

This modern medium is British. I've seen her work a bit on TV, and I've been really impressed. What can I say? I just *like* this person. (I never met her; we've never spoken, maybe we never will.) But I feel something going on in her that's just charming and caring and smart and able. One day I may check into her teaching work at the Omega Institute, in Rhinebeck, New York, and at Lily Dale (New York). Meantime, I just feel I can relate to her, and if there are chances ahead to catch her on American "telly," I sure will.

* * *

Finally, I do know that there are others working as mediums today. The late and sometimes discredited Sylvia Browne comes to mind. Tyler Henry ("The Hollywood Medium") comes to mind. James Van Praagh comes to mind. John Holland comes to mind. (Look for his book, *Bridging Two Realms*.) But I'm sorry. I just don't know enough about these folks to say anything helpful about them. And there are probably others out there who haven't even come near my awareness yet. But if you look online at websites, and if you go to where books are sold, you can check out much of the available public information on today's mediums and their various gifts. No doubt you'll find even more people I don't even know enough about to mention.

Again, I just want to say here that this book isn't designed to be the complete go-to book on the subject of spirit communication. I can tell you only what I can know for sure. Well, that is, as sure as I can be about this stuff, based on my own experiences. And the fact that the folks I do talk about in this chapter have all stood the test of time and my own scrutiny? Well, that may be its own recommendation.

Please understand, though: anybody who claims to be able to do a bunch of *different* things? Well, I'm going to have my doubts. I mean, I want a brain surgeon who only works on brains and not a guy who also removes corns. See, there are quite specific lines separating astrology and psychometry and tarot and palm reading and mediumship and crystal gazing, and all the other things people are offering out there today. But I have to say here that most of these require serious study and years of work. I mean, I spent four years just learning tarot before I felt ready to meet the general public, never mind charge people money. So, I just can't imagine being able to do what I do *and* do anything else equally well. Maybe some can, but I have my doubts.

Psychology and Spiritualism

Here I have to talk about something I read recently in the Introduction to Dr. Carl Jung's *The Red Book*. In his Introduction, Sonu Shamdasani tells us of Jung, the eminent psychoanalyst: "Jung's medical dissertation focused on the psychogenesis of spiritualistic phenomena, in the form of an analysis of his séances with Helena Preiswerk."

We're told that this interest was based on a study by Théodore Fluornoy and that through the work of scientists like Fluornoy, William James, and Frederick Myers, ". . . mediums became an important subject of the new psychology."

In the dissertation, according to the Introduction of his own book, *Psychology and the Occult*, Jung describes "several clinical cases of double consciousness, twilight states, and somnambulism." Then he presents in detail the case of a teenage girl medium, whose "séances he witnessed in the mid-1890s."

After this, all his life Jung worked to distinguish between mental illness and true parapsychological events. At the age of twenty-two he was already convinced that "the soul is immortal and intelligent and *not subject to the laws of time and space*. He declared the reality of spirits and spiritualism."

In her collection of essays, *Was C. G. Jung a Mystic?* Aniela Jaffé quotes Jung (from his own work, *Memories, Dreams, Reflections*): "There are parapsychological phenomena, for example, extra-sensory perceptions, prophetic dreams, premonitions, etc., which indicate that the soul reaches at least partly into that transcendent sphere," and that "it shares in a form of being which is outside time and space." It possesses, according to Jung, "a partly eternal quality."

Such courage! No doubt this eminent man was ridiculed *a lot* for believing in this "stuff." (As I said earlier, it was Dr. Jung who was my own courage and inspiration forty years ago for daring to explore mystical and parapsychological things, despite people ridiculing me too.)

If you want your own adventure, check out the amazing mystical *and* scientific writing and YouTube interviews of Dr. Carl Jung, the pioneer whose life and work have led me to where I am today. I'm grateful beyond words to this man.

And here I can also point you in the direction of a relatively new field, Transpersonal Psychology, and the work of Dr. Stanislav Grof. *Other Lives, Other Selves* is a book by Grof's psychotherapist student, Roger J. Woolger. The writer gives a thorough and balanced look at the idea of past lives, the memory of past lives, the ability to recall memories of past lives. And, most important, how all this is different from being aware of the events in *this* life (which I myself believe are the *only* triggers for emotional disorder). There are also Grof interviews on YouTube.

Chapter Seven

When the Spirits Reach Out

In 1941, Noël Coward's stage play, *Blithe Spirit,* premiered at a West End theater in London. The story involves a writer looking for material for his next book. He decides it will be about spirit communication. (Remember, it's meant to be a joke. The play is a comedy.) In the play, this writer-character invites an eccentric French medium (the hilarious Madame Arcati) to conduct a séance at his house . . . and he ends up being haunted afterward by his devilishly annoying and temperamental ex-wife, Elvira.

The play was a huge success and is still read to this day. But I doubt it had much effect on the mores and attitudes of London at the time. It was meant to be funny, which it is. But we get no impression that Coward was a "believer." Elvira just shows up, and we understand pretty quick that she has unfinished business with her ex! More than anything, what we can take from this is that the audience of the day wouldn't reject such a plot. Clearly, spirit visitation was accepted back then as a workable foundation for a play.

Fast-forward now to my own work with tarot over the past three decades. Well, I can tell you for sure that in tens of thousands of client readings, my sense that a spirit was showing up has kicked in *maybe* five times. Total. (And for sure, no nasty Elviras in the group!)

The best experience I've had in this regard? I was doing a reading for a female client, and I could "almost see" a woman standing behind her. I felt that the woman was surrounded by some kind of light, although I couldn't actually see the figure or the light. I told the client that somebody seemed to be standing behind her and that it was a female saying, *baklava*.

My client said, "Oh, that's my grandmother. She loved *baklava*."

Well, it turns out that the two were especially close in life. So I was able to tell my client with a sense of certainty that her grandmother was around and watching over her (which is what I felt at the time about the "visit").

This has been the *one* experience during a reading involving a spirit visit that I'm *sure* of in over thirty-five years. And I'm only sure because of that word. I "heard" it spoken in my head, and my client confirmed it. *Baklava*.

As I said, I like to have *physical proof* of things.

As for the other few experiences like that? Each time one happened, I was getting the impression *from the cards* that a spirit wanted to give the client a specific message. When I delivered what I thought was a message from the person I thought I was seeing in the cards, the client was able to tell me, yes. That was the kind of thing the deceased person used to say and think and advise. And the client would also be able to confirm a close relationship with the person I was sensing (grandmother, grandfather . . . specific relationships like that).

The one other category of "visitation" (just a handful, to be sure) have been the spirits who in life weren't nice and their watching over job is a kind of atonement. As if they can't move on until they make up for serious lacking in the love department when on Earth. (This makes so much sense to me, related to the idea that if we had a big enough overview of life, we would see there is balance after all.)

But other than the small number of times that spirits have seemed to show up during readings, I'm just a pretty normal psychic dealing with the living, not a medium dealing with the departed.

Outside my working life, though, things *have* happened over the years to tell me that spirits are in fact reaching out to me. But these things, I find, happen to a lot of people. They just don't pick up on it

In early June 2021, I wondered if great artistic gifts stay with us into the afterlife. A few days later, this incredible bird appeared on the floor, made by Amedeo Modigliani with a length of chain. Frankly, I was shocked, because to this point, he'd been forming simple line designs, "talking," but there were no perfectly recognizable, beautiful pictures. Now there is. Question asked and answered. We "spoke."

Early on, when I realized it was Modigliani visiting me and using string and yarn to communicate ideas, I asked him mentally for a clue. *If* we knew each other at another time, when did we know each other? The next morning, I awoke to find the "S" on the floor. The morning after that, I awoke to find the "V." Then I read that the artist's surrogate mother in Paris at the end of his life was Maurice Utrillo's mother, Suzanne Valadon. She comforted Modigliani in his last days. This may be as close as I get to knowing when Modigliani and I may have been together, if not learning who I was.

A few months before my dentist suggested I try yoga to relax (I was doing a number on my teeth in my sleep thanks to the pandemic), this image appeared on the floor. I thought it resembled the lotus pose popular in yoga. Now I realize this was just one more instance of Modigliani *anticipating* what would happen and *telling* me what I need to know. (It must be really frustrating for him when he's right and I'm clueless . . .)

Somewhere around 2019, I said to Modigliani, mentally, that it must be pretty easy to paint a seagull in flight. The next morning, there it was. And I'm not sure to this day if I'm more stunned by the images than the mental communication itself.

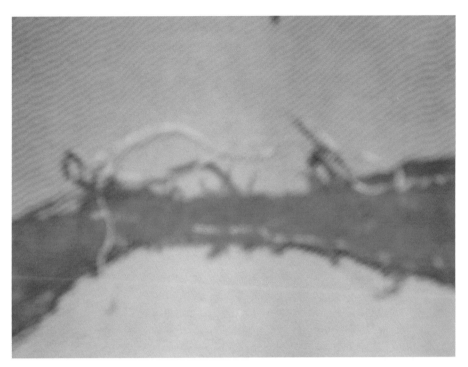

This is a (terrible) photo of the red belt after I had repaired it twice. Modigliani nightly lifted the belt from the robe loops as the robe lay on my bed, and I figure he was using the same spot on the belt every time . . . because some kind of energy (I think) was fraying the belt right there and nowhere else. I repaired the first spot. After that, a *different* spot started fraying. I repaired that too. And then *he* got the idea to use string on the floor, and I went along. Clearly, I am not the leader in this relationship of ours. I just feel blessed to understand what he wants many times and to be able to cooperate.

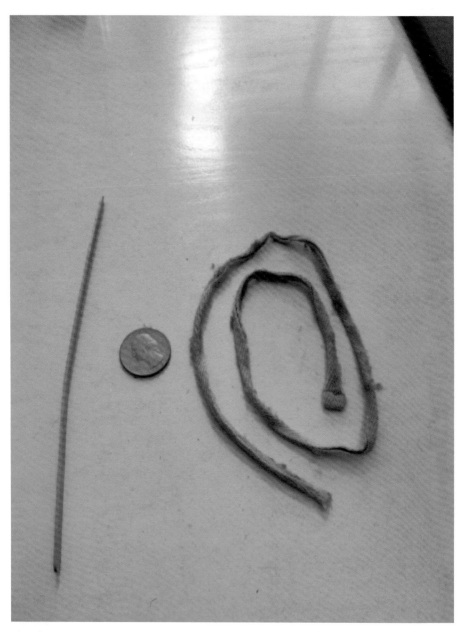

The drawstring was unknotted and removed from my pajamas (from under a sheet, a blanket and a heavy robe). I awoke to find it laced in my hair. It came to me right away that this was a gentle, childlike gesture. I haven't changed that opinion.

The quarter fell into my lap while I was eating dinner. It came from under the table.

The curved coffee stirrer appeared on the floor a few weeks *before* I broke a bone in my hand and needed a cast. The curve of the stick matched exactly the curve of the cast, which meant I could scratch away happily, thanks to the precognition of my "roommate."

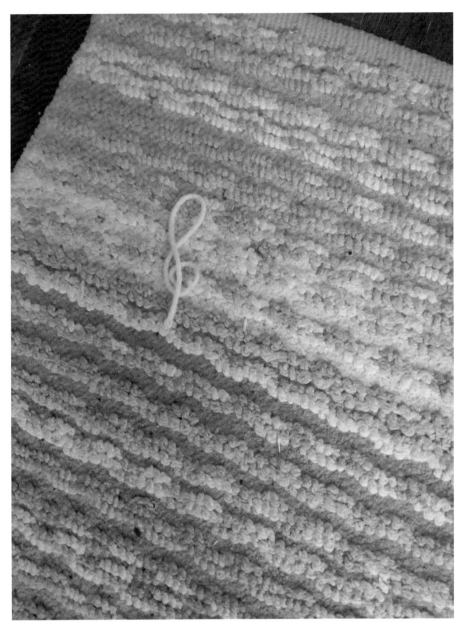

This is the *second* time this musical symbol has appeared. The image was placed across the room, a couple of minutes after I pointed out to Modigliani, on YouTube, a music video called "Amadeus." When I saw this new image, I knew it was confirming my guess, years before, that Amedeo Modigliani was trying to *identify himself* as best he could that first night. (Really, the only thing I knew about this man when he first came was that he painted women with long necks.)

In 2017/2018, when I was finally kind of driven to read everything I could get my hands on about Modigliani, I found a wonderful bio by Pierre Sichel. As I was reading, over time I started to notice an image appearing in a slender marble strip between my bathroom and hallway. The image continued to expand (maybe in the same way an artist develops a painting?). It was hard to trace the thing fully without ruining the stone (and this is a rental apartment). I did the head and neck and the suggestion of décolletage and dress neckline. (Modigliani had dreamed of sculpting in marble like his hero, Michelangelo, but he had lung problems and TB, so the marble dust would've killed him.)

if they're not open and aware, and if they don't have any kind of belief that it's possible.

So, to some of my own events:

Crow

The first time "crow" came to me, it was in summer in the mid-1990s. That afternoon I was in Barryville, in the Catskill Mountains, standing hip-deep in the lake up the dirt road from my house. I remember being mesmerized by all the fish swimming around my legs and feet. (The water of York Lake is crystal clear.) I was pretty much oblivious to the rest of the world. It was just as peaceful as you can imagine.

Suddenly, CAW! CAW! CAW! a huge and raucous noise broke through my reverie. It was coming from across the lake. Startled, I looked up, and at eye level I was seeing a crow flying past me out there. The bird was looking directly at me, and "yelling." It seemed as if the message was urgent (no, I have no idea why I understood *that*). Anyway, this moved me to look around. And there, to my left, maybe twenty feet away, a brown-headed snake was swimming right toward me. Man, did I run! I think I never got out of water so fast in my life. And, look, I'm not going to pretend I know anything about that snake. I have no idea what it was or what a bite could do to a person, if anything. But I do know what started happening after that.

For about ten years after that, whenever something bad was about to happen (particularly bad news arriving), I'd hear a crow caw three times, clear as day, in that same abrupt manner. And this includes one morning when the sound came from outside my tenth-floor window in midtown Manhattan. (There are no trees here, never mind birds.) Still, I heard that bird loud and clear, and I just knew something bad was coming toward me. A few hours later, I got the terrible news I'd been fearing for several years. The man I loved had died.

Now I think that "crow" was sent to prepare me for a bunch of lousy things. Maybe to provide a kind of protection, so nothing could "sneak up" on me anymore.

But I also discovered that negativity wasn't the extent of "his" language. I realized after a while that two caws means all is well or "hello." Five or six means something funny is about to happen.

The best example of "funny"? I'm walking toward the East Hampton, Long Island, library when in a tree nearby a crow starts "laughing." I say, out loud, "So what's so funny?"

Five minutes later, I walk into the library and I come upon a woman sitting on a couch reading *Crows*, the Ted Hughes poetry collection I had at home and autographed. But it gets one step better: it turns out the woman is visiting Long Island from Amherst, Massachusetts—where I used to live.

Trust me, yes, the whole thing *was* totally "funny."

So I have to admit it. I felt pretty bad the day I realized that "crow" had stopped visiting me. Maybe I didn't need to be prepared for bad surprises anymore? Maybe whoever sent this bird in the first place saw that I was finally on an even keel emotionally? Maybe I didn't need birds to get me to laugh again?

Well, whatever the reason was for "crow" coming into my life in the first place, I'm just so grateful it happened at all. And now I figure that if I'm ever meant to know what that was all about, well, that will come to me too.

At this point, I have to say this: The crow is a traditional symbol of a bridge between heaven and earth. *Atziluth* is a "word bridge" connecting heaven and earth. And what I do as a psychic a lot of the time works as a bridge between people and their spiritual life. I have to figure "crow" is my totem, the Earthly emblem of my own spirit.

The Duck

In an issue of *Psi Review,* I came across this story:

"In the Freiburg Zoo in Germany stands a serious monument commemorating the psychic feats of a duck!" It seems that late in World War II, Allied bombers were conducting sorties inside Germany, and the flight path took them over the city of Freiburg. The planes never bombed there. But in April 1945, that changed. One day that month, a duck at the Zoo began acting crazy . . . really crazy . . . when the air raid sounded its usual alert. And the people got the "message." *This time* was different, and they ran for the air raid shelters for the first time. That was the day the Allies finally dropped their bombs on Freiburg. The people were saved. Sadly, their messenger duck was killed. (Yes, I agree that it's quite a leap from duck antics to warning, but it seems the people made the leap, and ran, and saved their lives. So who's to say . . .)

Sherri and the Butterfly

One of my clients, a beautiful person, passed away a few years ago. She left me a little necklace in her will, and I figured I should have it appraised because she had many fine things. It was a lovely summer afternoon when I walked up Lexington Avenue to the neighborhood where she'd lived. I was going to the shop where she'd bought the necklace.

At the shop, I discovered that the woman behind the counter had thought as much of Sherri as I had. They'd been friends. We spent a while saying wonderful and true things about her and what the loss meant to us.

Now, this jewelry shop is in a brick building. When I walked out the door and turned left to head back downtown, something happened. Out of the side of the building, out of the *brick*, flew a tiny white butterfly. Right in front of me. Somehow, I knew in an instant it was sent by the woman who had passed on. (I mean, out of a solid brick wall?) The butterfly then flew down the sidewalk about a block, then across the street and up toward where Sherri used to live. Then I lost sight of it.

A week later, at a cross street near my apartment, a little white butterfly again appeared. Flew around me. Then flew away. The numbers of the intersecting streets (Manhattan has numbered streets) had such significance for her life that I sent an email to her brother to be on the lookout for a little white butterfly.

And maybe a month after that, I was stepping over a puddle at a curb. I saw a MetroCard in the water, dirty and wet. (MetroCards are used in New York to pay for subways and buses. Money's loaded into them and eventually used up.) Well, I wasn't going to stop. I mean, dirty water . . . But right then, a little white butterfly came out of nowhere and flew around me and left. So, I went back and got the card. Which turned out to have $45.00 worth of rides left on it. It was yet another gift from Sherri.

When I went to see Jeffrey Wands a few years later, I told him that this woman sends me a white butterfly. A split second and then he said, "A very little one."

Yes, Jeff, a very little one.

So, thank you, Sherri, for reminding me that we don't ever go very far, and there may always be a way to reach back afterwards.

Dragonfly
In 1991, I lost the love of my life. We'd met on August 2, ten years before, but he got sick soon after that. He never recovered.

It was now the early 2000s, and I had a little place in East Hampton, New York. My old Toyota was parked in the driveway.

One summer afternoon as I walked past the car, a dragonfly came and perched at the top of the radio antenna. There was no water anywhere near my yard. (This insect tends to be around water.) And I'd never seen a dragonfly near my yard before.

But it was August 2.

Still, it took me a second to make the connection. Jim had once shown me a letter his daughter had written to him. On the outside of the envelope, around the flap, she'd printed: "What planet do the dragons live on, Daddy?" And he treasured that letter.

I got it: the dragonfly was from him.

And this is the thing: I stood within a couple of *inches* of this insect. I was so close he could feel my breath. Yet he stayed. A *long* time. Then he decided to fly away, and I stayed there, watching him go. So, he came back. And again, he was inches from me, on top of the radio antenna. Fearless.

Then there were no more dragonflies until the summer of 2018. One day, on Park Avenue in the mid-thirties in Manhattan, I was walking past a small black wrought iron fence. A dragonfly landed atop the fencepost. Once again, I was able to stand thisclose and, still, the dragonfly stayed. Once again, our eyes were inches apart. Once again, there was no fear.

What more can I say? That day was August 2 too.

Dr. Dyer and His Butterfly
The late and eminently wise Dr. Wayne Dyer tells a wonderful story. He's in Hawaii. A monarch butterfly lands on his finger and basically stays there for hours. Stays, despite even a stiff wind when the trades blow in. The story is part of one of Dyer's TV presentations, and I encourage you all to look for it. His enthusiasm in telling the story is boundless. So, it seems, was the butterfly's enthusiasm in hanging in.

The Moth
This happened a year after I finished the first draft of this book. At the time, I had no idea Deepak Chopra had described Carlos Castaneda as "one of the most profound and influential thinkers" of the 20th century. I only know this now because it's written on the back of a book by Castaneda called, *Tales of Power*.

I came across the book (printed in 1974) on a shelf in a used bookstore where it wasn't supposed to be. And this reminded me I had read Castaneda in the 1970s. He writes of magic and sorcery and a Mexican Yaqui Indian master sorcerer-teacher named Don Juan.

The book was on my table for a week.

Four days after I bought the book, a large moth flew into my apartment. (Remember: 10th floor, midtown Manhattan.) I tried to encourage the moth to leave. No luck. The moth flew to where the wall meets the ceiling and stayed there. Well, after a while I went to bed, figuring the creature could find its way back out the wide-open window.

When I awoke in the morning, the moth was gone from the wall. But a few hours later, there it was again, flitting around. I awoke, and it appeared again and landed right away on the *I Ching*, on my bookcase. From there, it flew to a place behind my couch.

I found this peculiar, so I opened the *I Ching* to see what I would read there "randomly." And what I read was a section on the student questioning the teacher.

I closed the book and put it back.

Five days later, I opened *Tales of Power* and began to read. And, my God, there, on page 17, I read: "Knowledge is a moth." And it turns out that this book describes a series of meetings when the student, Castaneda, met with and asked questions of his Yaqui teacher.

Look, this was an *actual* moth. I mean, maybe I could imagine I dreamed it. But, no, it was a real moth, symbol of knowledge, who landed on the *I Ching*, one of the world's greatest sources of wisdom.

I stand in awe of everything I do not know about this universe. This one made me cry.

"Open Windows!, Open Windows!, Open Windows!"
A few years ago, I was sitting at the kitchen table in a little apartment in St. Pete, Florida, where I was spending the winter. At the time, I was helping somebody in New York with his business and telecommuting via computer.

(My computer is a Mac, which doesn't use the Windows operating system.)

In the little dining area where I was sitting, there was a window about three feet away. It was closed at the time.

Now, as it happens, the year before I'd seen kind of a shadow of a man standing quietly in that area. It was just a glimpse. I felt he was looking at me, but not in any mean way. And since many others in that building reported seeing all kinds of spirit phenomena there, I didn't doubt my "eyes."

Anyway, now I was working at my computer. And suddenly the whole thing just froze. The images on the desktop disappeared. And on the screen, over and over and over flashed, *"Open Windows!"*

I couldn't power the machine off. I couldn't force-quit the thing. Nothing I tried worked. And I couldn't do my job without it, never mind my writing.

I brought the computer to the Mac experts up the street. They took one look and told me that in twenty years of business they'd never seen anything like it. They pretty much said that what was going on was technically impossible. In the end, to restore the computer function, the techs had to empty the entire computer, delete the operating system, reload everything they'd removed, and upgrade whatever. These guys were at a loss. But they did manage to get me going again.

When I got back home, I had a brainstorm.

I opened the window! And I asked the spirit to please stop crashing my computer. I asked for him to please find a better (and cheaper way) to talk to me.

Long story short: *Open Windows!* has never returned, and it's been three years now. A year after that, though, a fellow resident and I were talking in my living room. She's what you'd call an "old soul." Suddenly, Catherine went still and was staring above me. She announced, mid-sentence: "Do you know there's somebody standing behind you?"

I said, "Tall guy?"

She said, "Yes."

I said, "I think he kind of lives here."

She said, "Yes, and has for a very long time."

Well, that building is nearly a hundred years old. It makes sense to me.

(As this book was going to press, CBS TV featured a bit by Steve Hartman about investigative reporter Brad Brown. Three days after Brown's mother passed away, his cell phone crashed, and the only thing he could get on the screen was a very blurry color image of a photo of his mother that was elsewhere on the phone. The online video report shows the image that appeared on Brown's phone. Which is beautiful, right? Brown is certain his mom crashed the phone and sent the image to tell him she lives on.)

The Dimes

Then, of course, there's the dimes.

One night at a bridge game, I mentioned I was writing this book. A woman at the table said, "A friend at work is always finding dimes. Do you know anything about that?"

Well, yes, as a matter of fact, I do.

See, for *years*, almost every day at some point, I was finding dimes. Heads-up. Shiny. And sometimes in impossible places for a coin to be. Once I found a dime nestled at the center of a "nest" formed by the roots of a little tree I was caring for in East Hampton. It looked as if that dime had been *placed* there. Really, I started to cry at the miracle of it all.

And when I mentioned this dime thing to Jeffrey Wands, he said, "That's your father. A dime used to be the price of a phone call."

Well, I had thought it might be my father at one point, because Franklin Roosevelt is on the dime these days, and my father was an FDR fanatic.

Then, back in St. Pete, I met a Long Island woman who'd had a reading years before with a medium as a member of a huge TV audience. DJ's brother, Johnny, had been killed in a car accident, and he "came through" that day. For a while before that, DJ and her husband were always finding dimes. Joe had been chalking it up to his own deceased father. But it occurred to me that it was Johnny leaving dimes for DJ, too.

I've also read about a lot of other people who wonder about all the dimes they're finding. Amazing, right?

This is kind of amusing: At one point a few years ago, I was really struggling financially. I found yet another dime. I looked at heaven and said, "If you're going to do this, why don't you just leave me green money?" Five minutes later I found, neatly folded on the sidewalk, five ten-dollar bills. (That was my father, too?) And, boy, I guess you do have to be careful what you wish for.

Then there's the quarters. *Two at a time*, side-by-side, heads-up. On three different occasions. In three totally different places. Well, twenty-five is 25, which adds to 7, which was my mom's birthday. And the first two quarters were exactly in the middle of a small intersection (believe it or not, Mystic Street and Park Street) under a full Moon in July. Well, Moon equals mother (trust me). July, the sign of Cancer, equals mother. And the numbers added up.

She was there for me. I had the proof in my hand. Two quarters. *Three times* this happened, in different places. I have zero doubt she was there.

So, these are the things I'm aware of so far when it comes to the spirit world reaching out.

Well, all but one thing, anyway. And I've decided to dedicate a chapter to this one other thing. Because it may be the single most significant thing of my life when it comes to being on the receiving end of kind-of heavenly communication.

You'll come to it later.

The Children Are Seeing

A few years ago, I came across a TV show called *Psychic Kids: Children of the Paranormal*. Of course, I stopped to see exactly what was going on here. And for once I discovered something wonderful. Despite the garish tabloid sensationalist ads for this show online, the fact is that it takes a serious look at an incredible phenomenon.

In the episode I watched, Chip Coffey (psychic/medium) and Lisa Miller (Columbia University clinical psychologist) were working with psychic children. Their job was to help the kids understand their gift(s). And to work with the families, to help them accept and embrace the unexpected way their kids are growing up: psychic, intuitive. Seeing and hearing the dead accurately. And scared silly by the whole thing.

In the episode I ended up watching, I saw a 13-year-old girl with a caring but strictly religious mother. Also, a 15-year-old boy with a caring and open-minded father. And a 15-year-old girl with a caring mother trying to understand her daughter. All the kids were living in their own heads. They were afraid to tell friends about their gift (curse). They were justifiably afraid of being shunned and ridiculed.

The team of Coffey and Miller decided to introduce these three kids *to each other*. Three kids from three different areas of the United States who otherwise would never have met. This experiment in *socializing* psychic children was a phenomenal success. All of a sudden, the girl who sees her dead grandmother was accepted totally by a girl who sees spirits in her house and a boy who sees and hears the dead speak. The three bonded tightly over just a few days.

How wonderful is this!

And it gets better. Because of certain experiences the kids had with the religious woman's deceased mother, she became open. She ended up deciding she'd let her daughter decide for herself whether she would follow the path of the Church or the spirit world. (Sadly, the mother may never see that *this doesn't have to be a choice*.) In just a few days: The girl was freed from her mother's rigid expectations.

The boy was just plain happy to know he wasn't alone in the world and could belong to a society of kids just like him. The third girl bonded with the other two and is no longer afraid of her own (haunted) house.

Frankly, this is a tremendously uplifting show. The subject matter is handled in a mature and intelligent way. The children are amazingly gifted.

For whatever reason, is it possible that these days an entire society of kids is being born with the incredible gift of *sight*? If so, we really need to learn how to accommodate them. Probably, we *need* them. For sure, they need us.

Chapter Eight

Devices and Methods

Over the years, mediums have used many different devices and techniques for reaching out to the spirit world (or for *saying* they do, anyway). For sure, the mental techniques require actual giftedness, and this involves talent possessed by what I believe are the rare few.

The physical methods involve using objects rather than abilities of the mind. And it sounds as if quite a lot of people could and still do use these things to make a very nice living, if nothing else.

I'm giving you all of these here in alphabetical order. (I'm noting which I feel are possible and which I feel are probably bogus.) I want you to have an idea of what some people can do and how they do it. I'm including things that don't necessarily have anything to do with contacting spirits, because they involve psychic ability. Again, this isn't necessarily the same as the gift of mediumship. A medium is a psychic; a psychic isn't necessarily a medium.

The exception to all this is the Ouija board. I do believe that maybe anybody can use this thing to contact somebody not of this Earth. But I also feel that we can't ever be certain who's going to be on the other end. And we can't control what they might tell us. See, I ask "A," and some unknown entity answers "B"? Maybe "B" is true? But only maybe.

So, to the list:

Astral Projection

I include this here because this technique involves letting one's spirit leave the body and go roaming around the universe. Then letting it back in afterward. Maybe some mediums in history have been able to do this. For sure, quite a few "ordinary" people have tried. These include Elvis Presley, Plato, Plutarch, Aristotle, Dante, and St. Paul. (And, yes, I said Elvis. Though I can't find a reference to it right now, I'm sure I once read that he was really interested in reaching out to his deceased twin. To do this, he was experimenting with out-of-body travel. And with meditation, which I've tacked on at the end of this chapter.)

Meanwhile, online I've found quite a few how-tos on techniques for projecting astrally. But, really, I doubt that just anybody can sit around and actually release his/her spirit for a period of time, never mind get it back.

Here's an example of a ridiculous online instruction:

Step 1: Focus on your breathing, control it, deep breaths in and out until you start to feel like your mind is emptying (*and maybe you also get dizzy from the breathing itself?*). Step 2: The vibrational stage (*say what??*). Step 3: Visualize yourself moving without moving. Step 4: Rise from your body (*just like that?*).

I admit: I'm including all this here to point out just how nuts some pursuits can be. There's just enough information here to make you *think* you can do this *miraculous* thing. But not enough to actually teach a darn thing. (The italics are my sarcasm bursting out. I guess I just can't help it.)

But, look, I also don't question that there *are* shamans and other spiritually elevated people who *can* do this thing. If you're interested, all I can say is check it out.

Automatic Writing

I've read that a lot of people can do this if they're in the right frame of mind, and if they don't consciously block it with skepticism or fear. Webster's defines *automatic writing* as "writing produced without conscious intention as if of telepathic or spiritualistic origin."

That sounds about right.

This method of communication attempt is so common now, Wiki even has a little how-to section on it (who knew!). The Wiki steps as follows:

- find a place free of distraction
- decide on how you will write (pencil, pen, crayon, keyboard)
- clear your mind
- call on the entity you wish to channel (*maybe you'd like to hear from a friend who's passed away, a spouse, a child, or you have nobody in mind and just want to see what happens*)
- close your eyes
- put your pen to the paper (or fingers on the keyboard)
- let your hands do what they want (*don't tell your fingers what to do; just try and see what happens if you don't focus on it*)

What I like most about this exercise is that creative people might be able to use it to break through "blocks." Maybe a writer can get an idea. We can attempt to use it to understand dreams. In these cases, whatever gets written (if anything) is coming from deep in the automatic writer's own mind. In this kind of exercise, the person with the pencil is the source. This doesn't make the result good or bad. The point is to get something useful out of doing it by bypassing the left brain (the part of the brain that thinks). The exercise is for talking to oneself.

But when it comes to using automatic writing to reach out to the spirit world, the purpose is entirely different. In that case, the automatic writing is acting as a bridge between a spirit and the writer.

It looks like automatic writing cropped up as a mediumistic device in the 1860s. It was used by many in their efforts to contact the dead on behalf of the living. (This method was used by some of the old-time mediums I told you about earlier. Maybe they were legit, maybe not. And it may be used today by some, but not relied on totally by a gifted medium.)

I have to confess: I myself haven't ever tried to do automatic writing. I'm not sure why. Maybe because I'm afraid of what will happen? I mean, let my hands do what they want? Hunh. Well, maybe someday I'll give it a shot. I mean, people do seem to survive the experience!

Then again, there was that *Atziluth* thing long ago . . .

Finally, Dr. Ian Stevenson published a good article on automatic writing. It appeared in the October 1978 issue of *The Journal of the American Society for Psychical Research*. If you can find it, you may be as impressed as I am at how careful Dr. Stevenson was in attributing automatic writing to the dead communicating through the living.

Camera

There have been amazing developments in photography in the past few decades. Today, it seems there are actually some digital cameras that can capture the images of spirits in the most surprising places. (Face it, though. Such an image popping up anywhere *would* be kind of a surprise, right?)

But in the early days of photography, the camera became yet another device for *contacting* spirits. At least, that's what the picture takers were saying. Most likely, though, *faked* photos were making a nice connection with the clients' wallets . . . and nothing more.

One of the most famous spirit photographers and his subject were Mary Todd Lincoln and William Mumler. He photographed the president's widow in 1872. He was already well known at the time. Mrs. Lincoln went to him incognito, to be sure he couldn't fake her husband's picture.

Well, it *is* possible that Mumler recognized her and doctored the picture accordingly.

But it's also possible he didn't, and that his photo is the real deal.

Mumler and his world of the spirit photography of the day are investigated and reported on in Peter Manseau's book, *The Apparitionists*.

From Errol Morris in the *New York Times*, we learn:

> "Mumler . . . is one of my favorite characters in the literature of the
> era. He took some of the most compelling spirit photographs of the
> 1860s that subjects swore contained images of their late beloved.
> The photos are compelling because of their weirdness; compelling
> because we, too, are *almost* seduced by the spirit images in them. We
> know that he was a fraud, but we don't know what kind of fraud.
> Self-deceived true believer, confidence man or a blend of both? And

the persistent mystery is, of course, *how* Mumler created these photographs. Do I believe in spirit photography? I blushingly confess I do not. I do not believe that spirits are recorded on photographic plates. But if we grant that this phenomenon does not result from some paranormal process, then how do we explain it?"

In the end, officials caught up with Mumler, and he was tried as a con-man. He was also acquitted, thanks mostly to the testimony of P. T. Barnum. (You know, the guy most associated with: "There's a sucker born every minute"?)

I have to tell you: I see the famous photo of Mary Todd Lincoln and the deceased Abraham *and* a deceased son, and I have to wonder about the truth of it. I mean, the spirits are SO clear and recognizable for who they were. It just makes me doubt the picture altogether. Others doubted back then, too. And because of the stature of Mr. Lincoln and his place in history, this photo was subjected to expert technical investigation. Some concluded the picture was genuine; others said not.

I can also refer you to *The Perfect Medium: Photography and the Occult*, another recent book, by French writers Chéroux *et. al.* This book contains 250 photo images from the Victorian era to the 1960s. All are supposed to be pictures of spirits and spirit phenomena. Well, maybe. Or maybe not.

But here's what I know for sure:

I went out in my neighborhood one day. I had an ordinary $29 plastic camera and ordinary film. This was in Murray Hill during the first snowfall after 9/11. I came away that day with thirty-two ordinary pictures of snow and wrought iron and buildings . . . and two pictures that defy explanation.

The one I want to talk about here:

Because of the darkness of the day, this 2001 color photo looks like black-and-white. And it's almost perfectly clear that we're looking at the head and partial face and shoulder of a woman wearing a dust cap (as they wore in the 1700s). Her white image is set against the very dark backdrop of a church. In her day, she would've been standing on land that was called "Inclenberg," the old Murray farm. (This was the property of Robert and Mary Murray, after which the neighborhood was named.) The woman appears in my photo against the background of The Church of the Incarnation, of all things. (I was looking for a shot of the planes of the roof with snow on them.) I have to tell you, I looked at the photo and didn't see her right away. She's a small part of a large image. But when I did notice her, I was stunned. She's there, clear as day. *Not* a foggy "spirit" picture, *not* vapor. This is an actual picture of part of a woman, against the backdrop of a church.

I started saying hello to this woman the day the pictures were developed. I was calling her "Mary."

Well, when I went to medium Jeffrey Wands, I told him the story. I said that I'd been calling her "Mary" for, like, sixteen years. He said, after a second's pause, "It's 'Margaret', but close enough." (And, look, this guy did *not* agree with everything I said that day. But about the existence of this woman and her name? He said, yes.)

Anyway, last week I happened to run into the rector of that church, a wonderful woman named Adrian. I brought her the photo. She couldn't believe it. She took a picture of my photo with her cell phone. And now she's showing it to people. That's how clear it is.

(Thank you, Margaret.)

This church was also the site of something maybe even more extraordinary. Very early in 2020, some of us were gathered there for a weekly meditation. As the last woman arrived, I saw she was with an older man. While she took a seat with the rest of us, he stopped, took off a raincoat, folded it neatly and laid it over the railing of a pew. He was a slight man with thinning straight white hair parted on the left. His long-sleeved white shirt was impeccably pressed, and I noticed thin lines running down and across making a large grid pattern. He wore no tie. After folding the coat, he hurried to a place a few chairs to my right, but by then I was focused on the sun-drenched stained glass across from me and I forgot about him. An hour later, I had to leave. I said my goodbyes to all to my left, and turned to the right to do the same with the old man. Who wasn't there. I was taken aback. I hadn't seen him leave. I asked, "Where's the older man who was sitting with us?" The replies were, "What old man?" and "There was no old man." I asked the last woman to arrive, "An older man didn't come in with you?" "No," she said. Then I thought, aha, the raincoat. But, no, no raincoat in sight, either. So, what happened is that day I saw an older man clear as day . . . who wasn't there. Again, this church has been for me the location of (so far) five "miracles," this one among them. The old man was as real and flesh-and-blood as all of us. But not.

So, then, to all of the rest of you out there: just keep clicking your shutters and filming your world and keeping your eyes and your minds wide open. You never know what's going to show up on film, or for real. Or who.

Clairaudience (a gift, to be sure)
This word refers to the ability of the medium to *hear* spirit voices. I do believe this can happen, though I don't know if anybody can hear the voices at will. Or if one can hear any physical sounds, for that matter. I do know that in the past two years, here in my apartment, all kinds of sounds have been happening. Something scraping the floor. A key being placed in the door lock. A slight banging in the air. A big crashing sound in the air. (Once, a noise woke me up, and I noticed that a painting that had been sitting on the floor had moved two inches to the right. Carefully, I put the painting back exactly where it had been. In the morning, it was now an inch to the left. And, no, I can't explain any of this, but I do know that many others have had similar experiences.)

Finally, I've become positive that none of the unusual sounds I've been hearing for the past two years are being caused by anything earthly in my apartment. And I've just come to accept it that noisy stuff happens . . .

Still, this doesn't mean I'm clairaudient. Probably I'd end up talking to Oprah if I ever managed to hear *with my ears* an actual voice *say* an actual word. (And trust me on this: I doubt very much I'll ever end up talking to Oprah or anybody else . . . Well, not for that, anyway.)

But in the Golden Age of Spiritualism, way back when, mediums regularly claimed to be hearing the voices of the deceased. Dead people who were supposedly speaking to them clear as day. And, occasionally, séance attendees could hear them as well, thanks of course to the shenanigans of the pretend-medium's confederates. It was common to have your crook friends hiding behind a curtain.

Clairsentience (another gift, to be sure)
It's said that if blessed with this gift, the medium can sense the presence of a spirit. The medium can feel the touch, can recognize a scent or fragrance, can sense the *personality* of the deceased. All this happens without the use of the actual physical senses.

As I wrote earlier, when I went to Port Washington, and while I was waiting in an empty room, the very clear odor of a hospice followed by the scent of flowers wafted past me. The smells were so clear I had to look around to see the source. But there was only a little flowerless bamboo plant in the corner.

I've been reading a lot since then. I've discovered that many people are able to smell things and identify them. And they're able to know who is connected with the aromas. And so they can figure out who are the people passing through. Look, maybe this is one of the greatest gifts we *all* have, but it only seems to surface for me once in a while. And maybe my few experiences with lovely aromas and unpleasant odors means that all of us at one moment or another can do it? Maybe we can all find the veil lifted and be directly connected with lost people and animals, in a fleeting sensory way? But still a very real way?

Clairvoyance (yet another gift)
With clairvoyance (clear seeing), one can see images, people, animals that are a symbolic way to identify the life of a spirit.

Webster's says this about *clairvoyance*: "1: the power or faculty of discerning objects not present to the senses; 2: the ability to perceive matters beyond the range of ordinary." The example given in the dictionary is: "The fortune-teller practices *clairvoyance* when she gazes into a crystal ball to see her client's future."

I believe that the medium I visited, Jeffrey Wands, has clairvoyance in spades. I got this from the way he described the people he was seeing in the room "with" us. For example, he was able to correctly identify my dear friend Angelos as a surgeon (and not "just" a doctor). I'm guessing he "saw" a scalpel.

And I want to say something about this kind of symbolism: When I was studying song writing, I learned about metonyms. This is a big word for a simple thing: you see a badge, you think police; you see a gavel, you think judge; you see a stethoscope, you think doctor. Like that. As a result, a lot of times we can figure out in the blink of an eye who people are just from their symbols. (I mean, if I say "stove-pipe hat," you'll probably think of Abraham Lincoln . . . if you're American, anyway.)

What the medium had to say to me that day was so much to absorb, it didn't even occur to me to ask him exactly what he was see-ing. But as I look back, I think this is how his mind probably works (accurately works, I might add).

So, if you take a sec to look around your own life and your own environment, you'll see that you *already* connect certain items with certain people and certain professions. If you're a creative person, this has got to be a great mind exercise to do. Then, if you lose some-body to death and "their" item surfaces somehow, well you can maybe know that person is paying you a visit.

Clairalience (you know, another gift)
This falls into the category of clairsentience and is also known as *clairolfaction* and *clairsentience*. The word refers to the ability to physically detect smells, aromas, odors. There's no physical source for the smells. It just seems that suddenly, in the air, there's a particular smell. Well, it's there to tell us a spirit is near. Usually, the scent we detect is asso-ciated with a particular person in our life. For example, Helen loved roses, and suddenly we smell roses. Joe loved hot bread, and we find ourselves detecting the aroma of hot bread. It's as if the spirit is aware that we'll associate a particular scent with him or her. And so we do. I've noticed this on a few occasions, and they seem to correspond to significant dates in the lives of the dead.

Claircognizance (my favorite)
This term refers to the psychic gift of "just knowing." You "just know" your boyfriend shouldn't get on that plane. You "just know" that somebody stole your dog. You "just know" you should go to a certain

place at a certain time and something good will happen. You "just know" not to go to work at the World Trade Center that day,

Actually, this is my favorite "*clair*" because it requires no outside, physical stimulus. Sometimes one does "just know." Usually, the "just knows" are our "little voices" . . . you know, the ones we tend to ignore all too often? And usually they're trying hard to warn us about something. It takes life experience and a great deal of trust to pay attention. But if you have enough positive experiences with your own "little voice" and your "just knowing," that kind of trust can develop.

And please note, you don't have to be psychic to hear your "little voice." You just have to be *human*! I think this gift is built into our biology somehow . . . like the hairs standing on the back of your neck when danger is near? Just like that, we're trying to tell ourselves something. Well, you know, if that's the case, we should at least listen!

(Along these lines, in *The Language of Tarot* I talk about my belief that psychic ability is *biological*.)

Crystal Ball

They say that in a pure crystal sphere, visions and images can appear. They say that somebody who can see these images can see them clearly. The process of seeing things in crystal, smoke, candle flames is called scrying.

Wikipedia tells us:

"A crystal ball, also known as an orbuculum, is a crystal or glass ball and a common fortune-telling object. It is generally associated with the performance of clairvoyance."

Well, if you've seen any movies or TV shows in the past half-century, at some point you've probably come across the scene. There is the bangled and bedecked "gypsy" woman peering into her crystal ball to tell the future for her paying client.

To cut to the chase, though: I don't know any credible psychic practitioners these days who'd use a crystal ball to see anything, never mind the future. Frankly, it all sounds rather theatrical at worst, and iffy at best. I don't mean to say that there's not even one person out there so gifted he/she can't see images in a sheet of Saran wrap. But, again, such a "seeing" person would have to be *gifted* to start with.

Along the same lines, my dear Greek friend, Vasso, long ago showed me how to "read the tea." This consisted of seeing the loose tea dreg "pictures" in the bottom of a cup after the liquid is gone. I have to suppose this is a kind of scrying. And I have to admit, I wasn't very good at it! Apparently, though, reading tea leaves has been around a long time all over the place. And the Chinese used to "cast" bones and yarrow stalks to divine the future. Again, this wasn't to connect to spirits particularly. It was to be psychic, which is a different thing.

To write this section, I looked into a brief history of using crystal balls for prophecy. I found that the ancient Druids are said to have used crystal to see the future. I also found that the use of the ball was big in Victorian times. And I won't go into it here, but Wikipedia has a "famous crystal balls in history" section that's kind of interesting.

As for my own ability to see using a crystal ball? I once had a job working for some quite wealthy people. The husband had a large, Victorian-era crystal ball on his desk. It was cradled in finely wrought metal that had greened with age. So of course, I tried. A couple of times. And I ended up seeing nothing that I could say had dimensions. I saw colors, reflections . . . but nothing else. It was pretty. But that's all.

Divining Rod

In his book, *The Divining Hand*, author Christopher Bird defines dowsing as searching " . . . for anything. This is generally done with the aid of a hand-held tool, like a forked stick, a pendulum bob on a string, L-shaped metal rods or a wooden or metal wand."

Most of us know dowsing from movie and TV scenes in which farmers use forked willow branches to search for water. When the stick dips toward the ground, water lies beneath. The practice seems to go back centuries. And some of us know from high school: when a needle is dangled above the belly of a pregnant woman, its movement is supposed to predict the gender of the unborn child. Straight back and forth for male, circular motion for female.

But back somewhere during the Golden Age of Spiritualism, the dowsing rod (divining rod) became yet another method for contacting spirits. (Yet another way to separate people from their money?)

So far, there's no proof one way or another of the usefulness of this exercise (naturally). And I have little faith in the idea of it as a mediumistic or psychic tool. Even today, "dowsing" has become a "thing" among aspiring psychics. Still, these folks usually need reference lists of things or maps or whatever for the rods to point at. And for sure they need to ask the right questions. (Remember, even a great X-ray in the hands of an incompetent won't tell you a damn trustworthy thing about your condition.)

Then again, in early 2021 I watched an Australian psychic on YouTube use dowsing rods to accurately predict our own presidential election outcome.

So once again I'm back to what I talk about in *The Language of Tarot*: success always depends a hundred percent on the ability of the person doing the thing. Otherwise, a tarot pack is just pieces of cardboard with cool color pictures on them. And a stick is just a stick.

Faraday Cage

Well, this is a far cry from "gypsy" hoopla, but there was a famous researcher named Dr. Andrija Puharich. Some acclaim him, while others say he was bogus. He was born in poverty in Chicago but raised himself up to acquire a medical degree.

At some point, Puharich was introduced to a book by theosophical writer Alice Bailey. The book was *Telepathy and the Etheric Vehicle*. And Puharich became seriously hooked on the idea. Could his mind really communicate with another mind? Well, the scientist in him wanted proof.

To try to get proof, he built two Faraday cages. These are copper "rooms" that don't allow the flow of electricity between them. In his early experiments with the cages, medium Eileen Garrett sat in one, another volunteer in the other. Their mission was to transmit thoughts to each other. It is said that these experiments proved to Puharich that information *can* be transmitted between two living brains. At least under the right conditions.

And when Eileen Garrett correctly diagnosed an illness for him, Puharich became even more interested in telepathy.

Ultimately, Dr. Puharich founded a group in Ossining, New York, called the Round Table. The group was dedicated to research into unknown worlds. They were especially interested in contacting an entity they called the Group of Nine. These are supposedly extraterrestrial "watchers" over the Earth and its people. Notably, the Round Table included President Franklin Roosevelt as well as Gene Roddenberry (yes, the *Star Trek* guy).

Some say that this group was successful in its mission. They actually did manage to contact the ancient Egyptian chief god, Atum. We're told that this god then communicated back to the group in a language of hieroglyphic symbols.

Meanwhile, volunteer medium Eileen Garrett was reporting: "His [Puharich's] aim is to reproduce by modern pharmacological, electronic, and physical methods the conditions used by the shamans for getting into a state of travelling clairvoyance and then, if he succeeds, to send people to explore systematically 'the Other World.'"

I include Puharich and his Faraday cage work here because I have to wonder how successful he might have been ultimately. I mean, if a great American president could be persuaded to be interested in this man and his ideas, maybe the sky was the limit?

Of course, Puharich's accomplishments are now ridiculed and/or disputed by many. But I like to think there's a grain of truth in what he was doing. Especially the part about blocking electricity so it couldn't affect his experiments. (This just makes sense to me, though I can't explain why.)

Andrija Puharich turned out to be a controversial *psi* investigator. He believed in psychic healing. He claimed to have witnessed this outside the United States. He believed that the human brain can act as a kind of radio sender and receiver. (I do, too.)

Well, we've all come a long way since his time in the mid-20th century. So maybe Dr. Puharich and his ideas merit a second look by serious people? Especially in light of Feynman's and others' work in physics, which I talked about earlier?

One curious thing more: an episode of *Perry Mason* used a cool plot that involved Puharich and his Faraday cage to expose a killer.

Ouija

In 1886, the *New York Daily Tribune* published an article about a "talking board" that had made an appearance in Ohio. The board was reported to be less than two feet square. Painted on it were the letters of the alphabet, the numbers, and the words "yes," "no," "good evening," and "goodnight." The board came with "a little table on little legs no more than four inches tall." (We call this table the planchette.) "The board was intended for use by the spirits to answer questions. Preferably, more than one person would place fingertips on the planchette and the "little table" would move, pointing to letters and numbers to spell out answers from the 'spirits.'"

The Ouija board was patented in 1891 by an enterprising guy named Elijah Bond. Smithsonian.com tells us: "Though truth in advertising is hard to come by, especially in products from the 19th century, the Ouija board *was* 'interesting and mysterious'; it actually *had* been 'proven' to work at the Patent Office before its patent was allowed to proceed; and today, even psychologists believe that it may offer a link between the known and the unknown."

Wait a minute! The *US Patent Office* tested this thing? Well, then, I guess I want to know what they did and how it worked and what happened. Maybe there's a file in Washington on this? If you're curious, too, I say go for it!

Anyway, the device was known and sold as a game, a toy for the masses. But it also came into serious use in the heyday of spiritualism as a tool for connecting medium to spirit. It's still sold today as a game. But I want to tell you that there isn't a lot that's fun about it.

For example? When I was seventeen and very, very stupid, I got my hands on one of these "games." And I asked, "When am I going to die?" (As I said: stupid.) That would've been in the early 1960s. The answer came back, "6 7." So now you need to know that until 1967 passed, I didn't feel completely safe. Then *age* 67 had to come and go before I felt I could rest easy.

It didn't even occur to me all that time that 6 7 was my mother's birthday. Had my own subconscious dictated the answer to the question? Or maybe some mean-spirited spirit had decided to "play" with me? (My mom was still alive and thriving at the time.)

So, let me say this: do NOT approach this device as a game. It is not. I think it *might* be fantastic for somebody who's had some kind of mental preparation and maybe also psychotherapy. And definitely also some kind of solid grounding in life. No, Ouija ain't a parlor game, despite its history and prevalence as such since Victorian times.

To be sure, I myself have no plan to ever again ask a question and use a Ouija board to try to get an answer! I think I just can't be trusted.

And if you'd like to read a stunning account of a claimed twenty-four-*year* experience with one spirit and a Ouija board, check out Professor Archie Roy's *A Sense of Something Strange*. In it, Roy goes into great detail about the appearance and work of Patience Worth. She's said to have "arrived" in the parlor of a Mrs. Pearl Curran in 1913 and stayed until 1937. During that time, this spirit dictated an astonishing three *million* words, including poems, prayers, and four novels. (One of the novels, *The Sorry Tale*, was published by Henry Holt and Company in 1917.) Patience Worth is by far the most famous of Ouija spirits. And from the sound of it, her fame is well-deserved. (I do plan to try to find that novel, which Roy says was a masterpiece of scholarship and "research" that even Mrs. Curran couldn't possibly have managed.)

Psychokinesis (PK) / Telekinesis
Webster's defines this as "movement of physical objects by the mind without use of physical means."

This idea has stuck in my mind for decades. I remember my father telling me: When he was very young, he'd stick a needle into a cork. He'd put a little paper arrow at the top of the needle. And then he'd spend hours trying to make that paper arrow move with his mind.

I never tried it. He said he never succeeded.

But I remember him also saying that he'd been influenced to try this by the Rosicrucians. (Brittanica.com tells us: "Rosicrucian, member of a worldwide brotherhood claiming to possess esoteric wisdom handed down from ancient times.")

Okay, I do confess to once doing something along the same lines. But it was definitely not as harmless. I was in my mid-teens when

I discovered that most of the time I could make somebody turn his/
her head just by staring and focusing really hard on the back of the
neck. It even worked when the person was far ahead of me and walking on the other side of the street. Ouch.

When it finally occurred to me that I could actually do this, and
that what I was really doing was some kind of mind control over others, I stopped. I didn't think at the time that this might have been
related to possible psychic ability. But I guess it sure might have been.

Anyway, in the Golden Age of Spiritualism, a lot of phonies were
out there. They'd supposedly make pianos dance and fly through the
air. They'd make sofas and tables rise and fall. Things would move
without strings attached.

The gift of telekinesis, you know.

But, of course, it wasn't so. There were *always* strings attached. As
any modern magician will tell you. Some of the greats today can make
things appear and disappear (or so it seems), even ginormous things,
right before our eyes. But all of them will be quick to say, "Hey, it's a
trick."

Back in the day, though, everybody pretended it was the real thing.
And everything moved, especially money.

The textbook, *An Introduction to Parapsychology*, (H. I. Irwin and
Caroline A. Watt) goes into some detail about the art of psychokinesis.
It talks about scientific experiments done in the 20th century to test
if the gift exists and to try and measure its effectiveness. The authors
examine cases in which strange things happen: books fall off shelves,
vases fall and break at the moment a distant loved one dies. And they
talk about psychic healing as a possible form of PK, although they say
this: ". . . according to some commentators, even conventional healing features psychokinetic factors . . . patients who believe prescribed
treatments will alleviate their illness often show an improvement
attributable to that belief . . ." And, "Mental processes are also known
to affect the immune system . . . On these grounds, the distinction
between psychic healing and other sorts of healing may be dubious."

Finally, Irwin and Watt discuss psychic photography as a possible
aspect of PK. They define the phenomenon as ". . . the psychokinetic
production of an image on unexposed film or photographic plates."

Slate Writing

The online Skeptic's Dictionary tells us this was nothing but a fraudulent parlor trick. The "medium" would usually use two slates (the kind used at the time by kids in school). One slate would be shown, clean. Then it would be somehow hidden. Then a second, identical slate would be introduced with a "message" on it. To do this well, I assume the "medium" had to practice a while to master the art of deflection. (If I call your attention over here, you won't notice what I'm doing over there.) But as in the world of fake psychics and phony mediums today, gullible people with deceased loved ones to contact were all too eager back then to have their attention called to wherever. Remember, we want *so much* to believe . . .

So that you can be clear on the difference between the work of a psychic and the work of a medium, this is medium Rebecca Rosen on oprah.com: "Simply put, psychics rely on their basic sense of intuition and psychic ability to gather information for the person being read. Mediums take it a step further. A medium uses his or her psychic or intuitive abilities to see the past, present and future events of a person by tuning into the spirit energy surrounding that person. This means mediums rely on the presence of non-physical energy outside of themselves for the information relevant to the person being read."

Spirit Hunting, 2022 Style

These days, technology has advanced to such a degree that there are machines for a whole lot of detecting that weren't available before. There are meters for sensing minute changes in temperature in a room. There are meters for detecting sound (electronic voice phenomena, EVP) and machines (oviluses) to analyze the components of sound. (Is it human speech, or is the house settling?) There are devices for registering movement across sensors placed in maybe sensitive areas. There are devices for measuring changes in light and electricity. There's the "ghost box," a two-way radio for use in communicating with spirits. (I've never seen one of these. I'd never even heard of the ghost box until I started researching for this book. I have no idea if it "works." But it's out there. So if you're curious, and have a few dollars to spend on it . . .)

* * *

Also, while researching this book, I came upon the diligent work of Gary Tillery. In his book, *The Seeker King: A Spiritual Biography of Elvis Presley*, Tillery tells a great story about Elvis's interest in Yogananda. ". . . the goal of the teachings was to establish harmony between a person's spirit, mind, and body. Elvis made a sincere effort to meditate and transform himself according to leader Daya Mata's suggestions."

The actor was filming *Harum Scarum* at the time. Tillery tells us that after Elvis's first visit to Daya Mata's California ashram, he returned to the site often for solace. He loved the sylvan setting, and he had an immediate rapport with Daya Mata. Tillery says, "In her features and demeanor, she reminded him of his mother. The more she described the aims of the Fellowship, the more excited he became. He said he was ready to turn his back on his career and join a monastery or start a commune. She advised him to go slow—that his development must be evolutionary." Tillery says the new student accepted the books she was giving him, but he was really enthusiastic to get moving. "'This higher level of spirituality is what I've been seeking my whole life', he told her. 'Now that I know where it is and how to achieve it, I want to teach it. I want to teach it to all my fans—to the whole world.'"

You know, the first time I heard Elvis sing "How Great Thou Art," it made me cry. The depth of the passion and something about his voice . . . well, I guess I "got it." I guess I *heard* what he was bringing to the table that day. His heart *and* soul. *This* was the music that would soothe him at the end of an insane day.

I think too many people dismiss Elvis Presley as the creation of his fans and his "colonel." Well, no, he wasn't just some kind of Hollywood fabrication, a puppet of the music business. Look, I remind you here. Not everything in life is as it seems, is it?

Chapter Nine

Pop Culture Paving the Way

Think about this: *Hamlet, Macbeth, Julius Caesar, Richard III*—just a few of Shakespeare's most famous plays, and in them what do we find? We find ghosts, is what. And, no, this great and revered writer wasn't the first to include articulate, menacing, thriving spirits in his plays. Actually, this ghost thing was popular with playwrights in general in those days, especially spirits coming back to Earth from "the undiscovered country" to stick it to one person or another. But maybe because of Shakespeare's all-around genius, his particular ghosts capture the modern imagination as much today as they did the imaginations of the theatergoers in his time?

Still, for centuries after the Bard, there was kind of a doldrums when it came to the spirit world in the popular culture. These doldrums settled heavily on the United States. I think this is because for centuries we Americans prided ourselves on being a practical people, on being industrious, hard working. I suppose we had little time for silly things like spirits and ghosts and psychics, never mind an attraction to mediumship.

And maybe this was also due in part to two savage world wars? Two conflicts that cost so many lives and did so much damage to our economy we were mostly decimated? And then, when we were finally getting back on our national feet, there was just no room left in a day for frivolous things? Or maybe the hiatus was in part due to the major

fleecing the bogus "mediums" did in the late 1800s and early 1900s. If
so, who could blame us for staying away from the proverbial hot stove?
I mean, once burned . . .

But it looks to me now as if the United States is doing a 180 when
it comes to belief in the spirit world and introducing that world back
into the popular culture, in films, on TV, and on the stage. In fact, on
October 25, 2019, IPSOS published a poll revealing that almost half
of all Americans (46 percent) now believe in the existence of spirits.
(IPSOS is a service that provides research to news organizations.)

Television

It looks to me as if this started happening somewhere in the 1990s.
I think this was thanks to the ever-spreading influence of TV and the
quickly growing presence of the Internet in mainstream America. It
seems that because of these technological mediums of communication, things of the spirit started rolling again.

On Manhattan Cable TV alone, for years in the 1990s, the
"Neighborhood Networks" carried metaphysical shows. These featured astrologers, astrology teachers, numerologists, tarot readers.
There were further sub-categories among the astrologers (horary,
Uranian, and such). Anyway, a lot of people doing this work populated the local airwaves for a while. (And I'm guessing that the good
ones were able to maintain a following off-TV, while the bad ones
ended up falling by the wayside.)

Anyway, you could see that folks were watching these shows with
active interest. People would call in with questions, and the TV folks
would do their thing and answer. Most of the time, I was sure that a
lot of what I was seeing and hearing was the real deal. And, for sure,
unlike when I got started in the psychic world in the 1970s, nobody
seemed to be ridiculing the TV people. At least not on the air.

Most important to me, though: All the folks doing these local
shows came across as compassionate and caring. They were out there
okay, yes, to promote themselves. But they were also out there to be
helpful to anybody who could get through on the phone. And from
the responses of most of the callers, I was able to decide that what most
of what the TV folks were saying and doing (for free) was right-on.

(In fact, from this array of MNN shows I discovered a truly great astrologer, Faith McInerney. She became my go-to person once a year for a while back then—my source for all things invisible yet knowable.)

As for network TV broadcasting across the country, I just have to talk here about *The Nanny*. If you've never seen this series, which ran from 1993 to 1999, you're missing something tremendous. This was television so clearly driven by love. It was TV that was determined to be nurturing and uplifting.

Anyway, somewhere in the last season I think it is, the widowed Dad is about to marry the Nanny. Over the seasons, she'd become a real mother to the three kids. The night before the wedding, Maxwell (the Dad) starts talking to his late wife, Sara. He needs her blessing on the upcoming wedding. And, suddenly, Sara is there. They talk. He's blissful that she's there with him. Finally, he asks her if she has any reservations about his marrying "Miss Fine." She says, "Who do you think sent her to you?"

Brilliant, beautiful, touching, comforting and, I think, *totally* real.

A little earlier, in the late 1980s, network TV treated us to *Highway to Heaven*. This show was the inspiration of lovely soul Michael Landon. It ran from 1984 to 1989. In this show, an angel on probation has to help people on Earth in order to earn his wings back.

Then, a few years later, *Touched by an Angel* made its appearance on American television. It ran from 1994 to 2003.

And in 1993, in an episode of *Matlock* called "The Ghost," the attorney is visited by a spirit seeking justice for his wife, who is on trial for his murder. No, this isn't a surprising plot these days, but what I saw was so authentic I have to mention it. Thanks to amazing writing and amazing acting, over the course of one hour I watched Ben Matlock move from fear to annoyance to anger to tolerance to belief . . . and finally to a kind of sadness, when at the end he realizes he will never see the spirit again. His character had become attached in a truly emotional way. And I can tell you, this *is* what happens. It was just the finest bit of acting, those last few seconds. No words needed.

To this day, you can see TV reruns of all these shows at least once a week. I believe these shows about spirit have a staying power that's as much about society's need for solace as their own intrinsic greatness.

Movies

Then one day there was also a turnabout in Hollywood subject matter. All of a sudden, it looks as if there was less hesitation to tell ghost stories in movies. Of course, the earlier filmmakers liked to focus on the idea that most of us love being scared to death and are willing to pay for the privilege. Still, not all of them did that. Some also told beautiful stories of love surviving death.

So, then, a very brief history of ghosts on celluloid (though they never said *spirits*) might go something like this:

Topper made its appearance in theaters in 1937, but no lasting ghost movie trend was started. A comedy TV series of the same name did show up in the 1950s, though, and it aired for a couple of years.

Then there was the 1947 movie, *The Ghost and Mrs. Muir.* This is a lovely *and* sad romantic comedy about the spirit of a dead sea captain and the woman who moves into his house. This film seems to have been the only one that featured humans interacting with spirits. (Although, in the late 1960s a successful series of the same name did show up on TV.)

And, oh sure, *Casper the Friendly Ghost* was flying around for a while, too. But this was an animated film. (I have to wonder if bankable stars didn't want to be associated with the stuff of spirits. So much reputation at stake, you know? So much to lose . . .)

As far as I can find, there was just a smattering of "ghost" movies between 1950 and 1990.

But then? Well then it looks as if the floodgates opened.

Here's a partial list of spirit-related US-made movies. Okay, *ghost*-related. But I really don't like that word, because it trivializes something really huge:

1961 – *The Innocents*
1963 – *The Haunting*
1973 – *Don't Look Now*
1979 – *The Amityville Horror*
1980 – *Somewhere in Time*
1982 – *Poltergeist*

1984 – *Ghostbusters*

1990 – *Ghost*

1998 – *What Dreams May Come* (this title is straight out of Shakespeare)

1999 – *The Sixth Sense* (the second largest grossing film that year!)

1999 – *Stir of Echoes*

2005 – *Ghost Whisperer* (a TV series)

2006 – *Silent Hill*

2007 – *Paranormal Activity* (the start of a film series)

2008 – *Lake Mungo*

2010 – *Hereafter*

2011 – *Grave Encounters*

2012 – *The Woman in Black*

2016 – *The Conjuring*

2016 – *Personal Shopper*

2017 – *A Ghost Story*

2021 – *Surviving Death* (Netflix documentary)

You can see from the dates how this thing seems to be snowballing lately. And all but one of these are just the American-made ghost/spirit films I'm aware of.

I can also say that this kind of film really didn't seem to start proliferating until around 2000. I have no idea why, of course. But it does have to mean that at some point Hollywood discovered there's gold in them thar hills when it comes to selling spirit movies to aspiring believers.

Remember? We want *so much* to believe . . .

The bottom line here is I think it's kind of like a circle. People start believing in what they can't see. And so, TV and movies jump on the bandwagon. And they make movies and TV shows that persuade even *more* people to believe what they can't see.

I guess we have to face it: in many ways we're all the product of our culture. And a lot of that culture is pop. (Like last week, when a foreign-born, middle-aged guy at my very conservative and traditional bridge game started *singing a Bon Jovi lyric* to punctuate a bad move . . . "Shot through the heart . . .")

With all this, I can only hope my theory is right. I can only hope that the spirits-welcome-in-our-culture thing is snowballing in a cause-and-effect cycle. Because if that's the case, then more and more people will start to believe in what they can't see or prove, and less and less people may ridicule what they can't understand.

Yes, it takes faith for such acceptance. But out of that can *come* faith.

And out of that can also come love.

As I said, a lifetime of this stuff can change a person.

Chapter Ten

The Near-Death Experience

Okay, I realize I'm opening up a big can of worms here, talking about something half the population doesn't accept, the other half does, and the third half have "been there, done that."

But I feel that if I don't do a bit on this subject, I won't be fulfilling the purpose of this book—which is to talk about humans connecting with spirits.

From the way things are described by people who claim to have had the near-death experience, I kind of get a big idea. I get the idea that at least some of our spirits can leave our injured bodies, can look down and see our bodies, and can look up and see the future. These people say we can see some kind of "light." We can see the shadows and forms of people waiting to welcome us and those of others basically "telling" us to go back, our time's not up.

Webster's defines this near-death awareness phenomenon in this way: "an occurrence in which a person comes very close to dying and has memories of a spiritual experience (such as meeting dead friends and family members or seeing a white light) during the time when death was near."

I have to point out here that the person doing the "traveling" isn't dead. Not in the medical sense at least. This, the doctors agree on. I mean, we can't be coming back to physical life once we leave it for good. Not without some kind of miracle anyway. This much I'm pretty sure about.

For the purpose of this chapter and to get as close to authorities on the subject as I could, I decided to do a little checking around. What do doctors and thinkers and philosophers and spiritual-type people think about the near-death experience phenomenon?

Dr. Oz

When I looked for a medical doctor willing to talk about the near-death experience, I found Dr. Oz. I discovered that in March 2016 he devoted an entire TV show to one woman's near-death experience. Her name is Anita Moorjani, and she used to be riddled with "lemon-size" tumors and afflicted with Hodgkin's lymphoma.

She tells Dr. Oz that, in February 2006, she lapsed into a coma and the doctors told her family "my organs were shutting down." The thing was, though, she could still see and hear everything going on around her "as if I had 360-degree peripheral vision."

And then she tells Dr. Oz she entered what she felt was "the most peaceful beautiful realm." There she started seeing people she knew. The first person she met was the spirit of her father. He told her that her "mission" wasn't done yet and she needed to come back to this world. She did.

The upshot of all this was that *five weeks* from the day she fell into a coma, Moorjani had zero tumors and no trace of the cancer that had almost killed her.

Well, I wonder if Moorjani's *true* "mission" wasn't to appear on national television and tell her story. Because if she did that, then others like me and Dr. Oz could repeat it. Because it's *really* important. But first, though, it had to happen . . .

Dr. Deepak Chopra

Doctor Deepak Chopra and Doctor Stuart Hameroff tell us that, because modern science cannot explain near-death and out-of-body experiences, it says these events can be attributed to illusions triggered by brain stimulation or to hallucinations due to lack of sufficient oxygen flow to the brain. They tell us that science tends to insult reports of NDEs/OBEs as unscientific folly. They add that this all comes despite the fact that **we cannot even explain *normal* consciousness in the first place.**

I've made the last part of that sentence bold because this seems to be really the most important thing you can say from a medical perspective. I mean, if we don't even know what is consciousness, how can we know what it's *not*?

The two doctors also tell us: "A Gallup poll estimated some *ten million* Americans have reported some form of NDE/OBE (Chopra 2006)." I've put two words in italics there because it's an astonishing number, right? And because scientists can't explain what *ten million* people are reporting, all those people must be wrong. Really??

Well so much for "science," if you ask me. At least in this case. I mean, come on! Even one million would be too much to dismiss, right? Or even just one . . .

For more from the collaboration of doctors Hameroff and Chopra on this amazing subject, visit choprafoundation.org. Here you'll find the fascinating piece: "End-of-Life Brain Activity—a Sign of the Soul?" where you can read this: "A quantum basis for consciousness also raises the scientific possibility of an afterlife, of an actual soul leaving the body and persisting as entangled fluctuations in quantum spacetime geometry. . ."

Yesss!! Entanglement. Spacetime. Soul. Somebody should be hashtagging all this! For sure, the point of this book . . . exactly.

Dr. Stephen Hawking
Speaking to students at Cambridge University (England), the late Dr. Hawking said that his years of research on the origins of the cosmos led him to identify a "strange" factor. He described it as "the God factor." He said that this thing doesn't work in accordance with the laws of physics. And it seems as if this was a new idea for Hawking. It marked a change in his previous opinion. Hawking himself said the change was related to the reported near-death experience of his own brother.

In Hawking's words (from *Body, Mind, & Spirit Magazine*):

"My brother has always been a role model for me. His rational, cunning and no non-sense mind has shaped my personality into the person I am today and has led me into the study of the fascinating world of physics."

Hawking goes on to say that after a serious accident his brother came back a changed man. "He has told me of the existence of a sentient being, of another world we mortals are unaware of, he has told me of God," he told the crowd. (We're also told the crowd were surprised to hear that from him.)

Hawking goes on, "Modern science relies on the perception that consciousness lies within the human brain, but what my brother experienced during his clinical death, I cannot explain. Does consciousness lie outside of the human body? Is the human brain just a receptor, capable of receiving the 'consciousness wave' as AM/FM radios receive radio waves? These are questions modern science has not yet answered and could redefine our view of the Universe and modern physics completely."

And so we're told that this ultimate scientist, Hawking, the theoretical physicist and cosmologist, said at the end of his life—thanks to a near-death experience—that he'd found what he believed to be a scientific basis for the existence of something the rest of us might call God.

Church / Religion
On the website, catholic.org, I find this story from Dr. Jeffrey Long. He is a physician specializing in radiation oncology who has served on the board of directors of the International Association for Near-Death Studies and remains actively involved in near-death experience research.

On June 29, 2016, Dr. Long wrote in the *Washington Post*, "Love is clearly an important part of near-death experiences."

He went on to say: "This experience of deep love often carries within it an affirmation of unity or oneness between all people or even all things. About four hundred people [who had undergone an NDE] volunteered answers to a long survey we offered, including this question: 'During your experience, did you encounter any specific information/awareness regarding love?'" The paper goes on to print some of the replies— from people who attributed their experiences, in incredibly moving words, to pure love and to God.

Granted, I doubt that all ten million people who may have had a near-death experience connected what happened to them to the presence of God, but clearly these religious folks totally did.

And bravo to a Catholic Church website for publishing this material.

Islam

I've found a page on Facebook that's been set up to record the reports of any practicing Muslims who can report near-death experiences. The page is *Islam and the Near-Death Experience*. The page was set up "to serve as a community forum to explore Islamic responses to the Near-Death Experience, a subject that began to gain significant traction after Dr. Raymond Moody published his book, *Life after Life*, in the 1970s." According to the Preface of this book, written by Dr. Elisabeth Kübler-Ross, "Dr. Moody inspired a first generation of researchers who have . . . in turn created a new science of near-death studies." While I see only five reports on the FB page (and a few comments on these reports), still I think this is significant, because the near-death experience doesn't exactly go along with the Muslim view of the afterlife.

So even here, change is afoot!

Other Points of View

I think Amir the Mashi (a screen name) sums things up perfectly when it comes to talking about people of a variety of faiths reporting near-death experiences. He comments on forums.catholic.com: "I've heard of people of all faiths (or lack thereof) having such experiences. It's not something exclusive to Christian—specifically Catholic—people."

Well, as a woman raised in the Catholic faith, I find this kind of funny. We Catholic kids would've been the *last* to be taught that the near-death experience is the real thing. I mean, I really can't imagine it. There's heaven and hell and purgatory and limbo, and that's it.

Or that's how it used to be, anyway. Clearly, the times they are a'changin.

Judaism

For the Jewish people, *olam ha-ba,* which means "the coming world," refers to the hereafter. Jews believe this time begins when our earthly life ends. Traditional Judaism teaches that death is not the end of our existence.

With this in mind, I searched. And I was able to find online this amazing woman (at chabad.org). Nomi Freeman is described here as the daughter of "the renowned Argentinian Kabbalist Professor Avraham Polichenco, of blessed memory. She is well known for her seminars on spirituality and Jewish mysticism. Mrs. Freeman has lectured extensively in Canada and abroad."

Mrs. Freeman tells us in a video that "I find it very inspiring" that many people are able to come back and share their near-death experience. She says that these experiences seem to be "custom-designed" for each person, although all seem to have the same "pattern." By this she means that what I'll see depends on who I am and what I believe when the experience takes place. Some see "other souls." Others are simply aware of "other souls." All venture into a tunnel at the end of which is a "beautiful and welcoming light." And all are eager to get to that light. She says each of us sees what we have to see in order to come back and tell the rest of us.

To do her study, Freeman read every report she could get her hands on, and she interviewed "as many people as I could." And then she started lecturing to groups. She says that "every single time" she gives a talk, somebody comes up to her and reports a near-death experience. An experience that he/she had, or one that occurred with somebody in the family. Their Jewish family.

Freeman estimates that five percent of the population of North America has had the experience.

Other Religions

It seems that Hindus, Buddhists, and such are already on board when it comes to accepting Near-Death Experience reports. But what

I wanted to do here is to give you kind of thumbnail commentary on the various religions and how they view the Near-Death Experience.

In fact, there's a major book out there by college educator Alan Segal. The book is called: *Life After Death: A History of the Afterlife in Western Religion.*

If you want to know more, you know what to do.

Passionate about Power Tools

Finally, I love this story. The History Channel aired a show in September 2019. This was about a year after I finished the first draft of this book.

The channel reported these stories:

In December 1992, Amy Tipping was a seventeen-year-old Atlanta girl. Suddenly, she couldn't breathe. The doctors thought it was pneumonia. But further tests revealed a tumor had compromised her liver and was pressing against her lungs.

Without a liver transplant, there was no hope.

Well, Amy was one of the lucky people who got a new liver. And, it would appear, with it came a whole new set of interests and personality traits. After the transplant, Amy found herself passionate about doing serious home renovation projects. Prior to the operation, she'd had zero interest in anything remotely like this. So a puzzled seventeen-year-old set out to learn about her donor.

Amy was told that her new liver had come from a man named James who'd been killed in a car accident. Through a microfilm search of local papers, she was able to discover that a man named James, age 47, was a policeman who'd died in a car accident just before her surgery. To her surprise, Amy also discovered that this James had loved working with power tools and doing major home renovation projects. Could *this* be why she was now really interested in doing work around her parents' house, like replacing flooring? Could this be why she also found herself with a reported "new" *personality and behavior* patterns?

Did James's liver somehow "remember"?

Another case reported by the History Channel is that of a young boy whose heart was donated to a factory worker. The boy had been killed by a car when he was coming from a classical violin lesson. And the worker? Well, he awoke from his surgery with a sudden, brand-new interest in classical music.

Did the boy's heart somehow "remember"?

Well, Dr. Gary Schwartz of the University of Arizona has a theory. He believes that our organs may "learn," right along with us. He thinks that if our brains can learn, maybe other organs can learn too. Frankly, I find this fabulous to imagine.

Then there's the work of Dr. Joyce Hawkes, who works with organ recipients. She has discovered that many develop personalities that match the personalities of their organ donors.

I hope that Dr. Schwartz and Dr. Hawkes and other researchers working along the same lines can come up with something definitive. And I hope it doesn't take too long. There are a LOT of transplants happening these days! As it is, there are tissue and blood match tests for both donor and recipient. But suppose we need to be doing more?

At first blush, this may all sound weird. But Amy Tipping's and the factory worker's stories aren't the only ones like this. Maybe one of you reading this might be interested enough take up the research mantle. There may be a great book in it.

As for why I include the subject here: If organs can retain personalities after death, what does that say about whole persons? Was ancient Greek thinker Pythagoras right? The *personality* may persist after death? There is a soul? The soul lives forever?

Well, yes. That's what I think, too.

And all we need is for science to be able to prove what right now many of us are taking on faith.

Meanwhile, the anecdotal evidence is piling up.

Chapter Eleven

Ordinary People, Extraordinary
Stories

As I was shaping this book, I had a brainstorm. I went online to craigslist.org and posted a request for stories:

> hi
>> for something i'm writing: if you have lost a loved one, and you feel the
>> loved one reached out to you after death, i would love to know the story.
>> if i repeat the story in the writing and you want to be anonymous, i can
>> honor that. thanks so much, jeannie reed

You can see I left the request kind of vague. I didn't want to put any specific ideas into anybody's head. I wanted only authentic stories from real people.

I interviewed all who replied. Some also sent the memory in writing and asked that I use their own words.

Here are some of the replies I received.

Dee and Bobby

Dee was seventy years old. It was New Year's Day, 2010. At eight in the morning, she went upstairs to wake her son, who lived with her in her "big old house." She found Bobby in his desk chair, his head on the desk. He had overdosed sometime in the night, maybe eight hours before. A Nirvana song lyric lay on the desk beside him. He was thirty-four years old. (Dee can't remember the name of the Nirvana song.)

Bobby's life had been hard. As a kid growing up, he'd been beaten and abused at home, but not by Dee, who loved him "so much." She said that for a while he had some kind of work "in the stock market—he was good with numbers," but "it didn't work out." But Dee said Bobby was a good-enough drummer to be called into Manhattan from New Jersey to fill in for band gigs here and there.

Dee told me that Bobby had been in pain pretty much his whole life. (And, yes, I know this to be true: emotional pain when young can lead to drug abuse when older. *Anything* to take that terrible deep heart hurt away.)

Anyway, she understood. So, when at some point Bobby graduated to heroin, she accepted it. He couldn't stop. That much she'd learned. She saw there was really nowhere else to go with it, except to love him and pray. The most she can manage now, on remembering the morning she found her son, is that it was "very upsetting."

Dee told me that Bobby had loved animals. "He was very sweet and helpful. He was very kind to animals. He loved cats."

So it came to pass that maybe three days after Bobby died, Dee had to go out to her backyard. All of a sudden, she told me, "A wild bird, a starling, flew around and then landed on my shoulder and stayed there."

She said, "I knew right away. I said, 'Bobby, that's you, isn't it? Are you all right?'" And so there she was, walking around her backyard with "this little bird" on her shoulder. At one point she had to go into the house. The bird flew away. She came back out, and the bird came back to her shoulder.

Soon after this, she said her friend Keith came to the house to check on her. She told me that Bobby and Keith liked each other. The little bird flew onto Keith's sweater. Keith "got scared, so I put my finger out, and the bird hopped onto it." Then one of Bobby's girlfriends drove up, and Dee went out to the car with the bird on her shoulder and said, "Look! Bobby's back."

Dee says the girl screamed and drove off fast. And that's when the starling finally flew away. As of the time of the interview, he had not come back.

Dee understands that her son loved her and didn't get a chance to say goodbye, and that now, somehow, he had.

After telling me this amazing story, she added that Bobby was a "good-looking man with a 123 IQ." I could hear the pride in her voice.

She said, finally, that she was telling me the story so that "Bobby will be remembered."

Dee also told me a couple of other stories, from which I take it that this taxi-driving New Jersey woman is kind of psychic. In one instance, she said, a man she'd been close to had left her and gone to Florida. At some point after that, "I heard his voice in my head saying, 'It's over, it's over, don't you understand it's over?'" She learned later that the man had died in Florida on the day she'd heard the voice and at the time it had spoken to her.

(Dee's wish is that Bobby be remembered. I have dedicated this book to them.)

Cecile and Chris

Cecile and her partner, Chris, met in mid-life. He'd had some serious health issues and needed a pacemaker. Cecile says that Chris worked to the end. He always arrived home to the house they shared by 6:00 PM. It was maybe a forty-five-minute drive from his job. He was a responsible man who cared a lot about Cecile.

She learned one day that Chris wasn't coming home. He'd left his car by the side of the road and died of a heart attack nearby.

These are her words: "The day after Chris passed, something told me to wash the clothes he'd worn during the week. After I put them in the dryer, I turned the knob to start the machine. I placed my hands on top of the dryer and asked Chris to give me some sign that he was still there with me. The dryer was running when I went back upstairs. When I got to the top of the landing, I heard what sounded like two high-pitched female voices and one male voice that were laughing. I tiptoed around the house to see where the sounds were coming from. When I returned to the living room, the sounds had stopped. The next day, I went down to the laundry room to retrieve the clothes from the dryer. They were soaking wet. I figured I must have forgotten to turn the dryer on. So, I set the timer again and hit the start button. The dryer was humming and I went back upstairs. When I checked the clothes a few hours later, they were still soaking wet. I asked my neighbor, a Sears appliance repairman, if he'd check the dryer. When he removed the bottom panel, he saw that the belt that turned the drum had exploded into little pieces."

She goes on:

"Chris died at 5:45 PM. The anniversary clock on the mantel stopped advancing beyond 6:00 o'clock. He usually drove into the driveway after work at 6:00 every day. The morning after Chris died, [I found that] the face of the clock had been turned to face the wall, and the time would just run from 6:00 o'clock back to 6:00 o'clock."

As with Dee, Cecile had another experience with a spirit:

"The year was 1964 or '65. I was selected to sing with the All-State Chorus. The concert was to be held in eastern Massachusetts. My host family were poor. They lived on the third floor in a rickety old tenement house. The family had a daughter about my age. I was 16 or 17 at the time. After a grueling day of rehearsal, we retired to our host families' homes. I got ready for bed and turned off the light. I settled into bed and pulled up the covers. As I tried to fall asleep, I heard sounds coming from the wall next to the bed. It was singing. Beautiful singing in four-part harmony. I recognized the language as Latin. I strained to keep awake so that I could keep listening. It sounded like angels that lulled me to sleep.

"The next morning, I told my new friend about my experience with hearing angels singing in the wall.

"She said, 'Don't say another word. Come into the kitchen and tell my mother what you just told me.'

"The mother was sitting at a very old wooden table in a dimly lighted kitchen. She was sipping a cup of coffee. My friend said, 'Tell her what you just told me.' I recounted my experience of hearing angels singing in the wall. Her mother started to cry. She used to hear angels singing in the wall too *and had been institutionalized* because 'they' (the family) thought she was nuts.

"I guess by the luck of the draw I ended up with that family, or maybe I was sent there for a purpose . . ."

(And please let me say here that I have no doubt that way too many people have been "institutionalized" just because they've been able to see and hear what the rest of us can't. This, to me, is a crime. A crime first of ignorance, then of power. I guess it's easier to label things we can't control (which is a fantasy in its own right), and things that maybe we also fear . . . So, this poor woman was shipped off to a mental hospital? Probably until she came to her "senses"? OMG.)

Jennifer and her Honey
In answer to my posting, Jennifer wrote:

"I actually saw my honey . . . maybe it could be called the dream state. He looked so bright and healthy. I used to cook for him every day when he was very ill. After he died, I saw a plate or saucer coming 'toward' me. This plate had a cup on it. It was sort of golden. This all occurred inwardly. I believe he was sending me a plate of spiritual food as a gift of love from one of the heavens. So, yes, I have met with him inwardly about three times until it was time for both of us to move on."

The thing about this story that leads me to believe all this as Jennifer believes it—though for sure I'm no expert—is that it happened "three times." And *then* there was acceptance and some kind of understanding about the process on Jennifer's part. Something about the number being so particular tells me it's real and not just something in Jennifer's imagination or "dream state." I believe, as she does, that her love came to see her before he moved on totally.

Harry and Amanda
Five years before we spoke on the phone, Harry had lost his wife, Amanda. Until she became ill, they'd had sort of a contentious marriage here and there, but some of the good times saw them playing tennis together.

After Amanda fell ill and after a first surgery, Harry would take her to their usual tennis court and gently lob balls her way, so she could at least swing at them. He did this at the end of the day when they'd be sure not to inconvenience other players.

Then, at the urging of her family, Amanda endured another surgery. This second operation took away Amanda's ability to stand and balance and see clearly. (Harry will always believe that her life was artificially prolonged as kind of a medical experiment, and that the prolonged life lost all quality. The lively and independent woman his love had been was gone.)

Finally, her cancer claimed her, and Amanda passed away.

Harry says that a few months after she died, he was at that tennis court. He was off-court unpacking his gear when he saw Amanda standing next to the net. "But by the time I could get to the spot, she was gone, and I felt like I had just missed her."

This kind of thing hadn't happened again by the time we spoke, although Harry said he always looked for Amanda around that court. At the time we spoke, the memory of the moment of her "visit" was as real to him as the reality had been at the time.

I need to say here that Harry spent a bit of time claiming to me that he didn't want to believe in a hereafter of *any* kind. He said he wanted to think we die, "and that's it."

But, of course, he does—he does want to believe.

DJ and Barbara and Johnny

This story is interesting to me for one major reason: I can't tell you how many times in the course of my own work I've said something to a client and he/she denies the truth of it. The client says that what I'm saying doesn't "click." The client shrugs. Until of course, an hour later (sometimes a few days), when the client gets in touch again and tells me I was "right." Suddenly, all is remembered.

This forgetting can even be about something really serious and important. And still, it won't "click" right away.

I attribute these lapses of memory to the serious emotional condition that people can be in during a psychic reading. It's as if they're being carried along on a cloud or something, and their logical minds just aren't working up to speed.

Yes, I suppose that maybe this isn't making sense. But it's the best I can do. Or how about this? Getting a good reading can be like being on a high. And you really don't want to come down. A few times I myself have had good readings and it's been kind of like being hypnotized. And for my clients, the images and colors of the cards probably go a long way to promoting this dream state in them.

So:

DJ says her brother was eighteen when he was killed in a traffic accident. She and her mother had no experience with him after that. They never felt he might be trying to reach them.

But maybe twenty years after Johnny's death, medium John Edward starting taping *Crossing Over*. DJ and her mother, Barbara, and Uncle John read about it and traveled into Manhattan to be in the audience. DJ tells me there were a lot of people there. She also says that Uncle John was totally skeptical and warned her and Barbara not to talk in line. "In case people are listening for information." They did as he suggested.

Anyway, it didn't take too long after the show started before DJ says Edward was zeroing in on the two women and asking specific questions. It seemed as if he just couldn't let go of anything. But I get the feeling, really, that it was *Johnny* who was doing the insisting, and Edward was kind of helpless. He was just a mouthpiece for a determined spirit speaker who wasn't going to be shut up!

DJ says this went on so long that she and her mother were finally embarrassed because they felt as if they were taking up the whole show. "Other people weren't getting a chance." But, hey, if it was her deceased *brother* doing all that, then what could all the living people do but just go along? She also says that she and her mom were both totally "emotional" through all of this. So I can understand that nothing was really registering with them. Logic was out the window.

See, the problem with how long it was taking. DJ and her mother kept *denying* everything Edward was saying. They just couldn't relate to it. No "click." So, Johnny was keeping it up. DJ says the three in her group eventually left the taping feeling as if nothing at all had happened.

Until a little time passed, that is, when things Edward had been insisting on did start to "click."

Long story short? Uncle John is no longer a skeptic. And DJ and Barbara are certain beyond a shadow of a doubt that Johnny was with them that day.

Jose and "Robert"
Jose wrote:

"I had an aunt who was going to give birth. Unfortunately, she had a miscarriage. Everyone was sad. Then one night I had a dream about the unborn kid (let's call him Robert). In this dream, he was a successful scientist who discovered the cure for cancer. I asked him the secret to success. He said, 'Be willing to fail many times. But with each passing time, learn why you failed. Then use this gained knowledge to tackle the problem once more.'

"At the time, I was failing classes in college and thought about quitting. The dream helped me realize that there are people watching my growth as a person, even the ones that never got a chance at life. It hit me at a spiritual level. And from then on, I decided to continue. No matter how much more time it will take to accomplish my dream, I will continue, even in failure.

I hope this inspires."

Terry and Mom
Terry writes: "At the beginning of the year, I had a dream about my Mother. She died thirty-five years ago. In this dream she was younger. She was happy, and she was sweeping this empty apartment with only two chairs in it. I was sitting in one, and some unknown person was sitting next to me. It looked like the floor was new. It was shining, it was wood. A dark brown. My mother said to me. 'Don't you worry, everything is going to be all right.'

"I was happy in the dream and happy to see her; I didn't see her as deceased. Then I woke up and I felt good."

(Terry tells me she had some bad and worrying health issues that year, but she was then in fact becoming "all right.")

Earlier, Terry had had other dreams, though she hadn't had one for a long time.

"One dream long ago: we were flying somewhere, but I never got to go with her. The pilot told me, 'You're not supposed to be on this plane.' Another time, I dreamed I was on the bus with my deceased aunt and cousin, and I had to get off for a moment, and when I tried to get back on the bus, a man crossed in front of me and said, 'It's not your time.'

"Another time, while I was asleep, the phone started ringing and wouldn't stop. I finally dragged myself out of bed to answer, but nobody was there." At which point, Terry says, the ceiling literally fell in on the bed. She called 911, and a fireman told her, 'It was your almighty on the phone calling you' . . . . He told me that if I had stayed in bed, I would've been dead."

Julian and Isabel

By today's standards, Julian was an abused child. At the time we spoke, he was fifty-seven, an electrician, and fully recovered from a longtime cocaine habit that "should have killed" him. He said he believed very much in a loving God. Julian's mom had died forty years before. And despite the fact that she was "very strict," he said the loss was "pretty devastating" for the nine-year-old kid he was. Seven years after that, Julian was "doing cocaine 24/7" and "I just couldn't stop, no matter how hard I prayed." (He said he credits his ultimate salvation to his wife, a woman he is convinced was "sent" to him "from the other side.")

When Julian was in his late thirties, shortly after marrying, he and his new wife moved from Rhode Island to Oregon. There, he had a dream. He was sure that this was a trip to "the other side," where there were "mountains of such glorious colors" that were "the most amazing in the world."

When Julian was about forty-five, he had reason to be really angry at somebody. He wanted to do real harm to the man. One night during this time, he had what he felt was a dreamless sleep, but when he woke up, "all the anger was gone." Then he had a second night like that and a second morning like the first.

And then Julian had a third dream. His mother was there. He told me he'd never dreamed about her before. "I was brought to her, and she was in her front garden, and we saw each other, and nothing was said, and all we did was hug and cry. It was the most amazing thing in the world. The love on the other side is the most incredible thing. And I couldn't stop crying for hours."

Lucille and Diane
Lucille writes:

"My sister, Diane, passed away nine years ago yesterday. I believe she sent me a sign or something. Here's my story:

"Whenever I play golf on a league day (Tuesdays or Fridays), I can't choose who I play with. The foursomes are assigned by the pro shop staff or the pro shop computer. Two weeks ago, one of the ladies in my foursome was a woman named Diane A. As we were getting to know each other, I found out that when she was first married, she lived in the same apartment complex as my husband John did when I met him. Even though she didn't live there at the same time he did, we were able to compare notes on the area and talk about the restaurants we frequented and things like that.

"The following Friday, I was teamed up with her again. Then this past Monday, John and I went downtown to the Christmas tree lighting celebration. We bumped into her and her husband amidst the hundreds of people on the streets of Naples!

"Yesterday, one of the random ladies in my foursome was Diane F. Usually, a foursome plays whatever the tournament is as a team, and team scores are used to determine the winners. But, yesterday, the tournament was a 'blind draw' tournament. This is one where the pro shop picks names at random and assigns everybody to somebody other than the people in their foursomes. You don't know who you're going to be paired with until the tournament is over and the results are posted. Well, my 'blind draw' match this time turned out to be *another* Diane. Diane S. We won first place. And I believe my sister was letting me know she was thinking of me and that she knows how much we all miss her.

"The next time this happened, yet another Diane showed up. This one arrived five minutes before tee time, cup of coffee in hand, and didn't even acknowledge me when I introduced myself. She simply said, 'It's too early!' So, I started out feeling pressured because she wasn't there on time. Then the woman proceeded to ignore me for most of the round, except for a few times when she said, 'Good shot.' There was never any chit-chat! She never even smiled! She occasionally spoke with one of the other players but totally ignored the fourth.

"I must say that I felt very uncomfortable playing with such an unfriendly person. Needless to say, none of us played well in our foursome, and we ended up coming in dead last! But in one respect, I had to laugh! It was as though my sister was looking down on me, laughing, and saying, 'You didn't think I was going to help you win again, did you?'"

(So *many* Dianes? What else could it be!)

Kelli and Dad
Kelli writes:

"It was in 2013, about five months after my dad died, when I was awakened by a large bright white light hovering in my bedroom doorway. The light was a blob, the edges of the form were milky, and it pulsated, and it was in that moment that I felt a frequency, a vibration, an energy that I never felt before. It overwhelmed me, and I sat up in bed calling out, 'Dad, is that you? You're scaring me.' The light came closer to the edge of my bed, and as it neared, the frequency intensified, the light grew bigger and the vibration began to take over the room. My body felt like it would explode, not into pieces but into sound.

"I kept calling to my dad, asking if it was him and to give me a sign that it was. I would've been comforted by his acknowledgment that he was there, but a vocal reply never came.

"Finally, the large white light turned toward the bedroom door. And I saw the back of my dad's body. He was in his robe and slippers. The slippers . . . they were going out the door.

"The light faded, the vibration faded, and then he was gone."

Marian and Jerry
Marian writes:

"My dear friend, Jerry, passed away in March 2002. Right away, I felt *very* strongly that he was coming to me. After a while, though, I felt he wasn't around me anymore.

Then, in 2003, about a year after I lost Jerry, I was having lunch with a friend in a diner on the Upper East Side. This was near Lenox Hill Hospital, where he passed away. There was fairly inaudible background music playing among the busy chatter of a heavy lunchtime crowd. I mentioned to my friend how close the diner was to the hospital, and she asked, 'Does Jerry still come and visit you?' I said, 'No, it appears that he's not around me anymore.'

"Well, no sooner had I said this than the background music went VERY loud for about thirty seconds. It was as if a hand had turned up the volume by ten times. The thing is that the music playing at that moment was a very obscure song from the '60s called "Many Rivers to Cross" by Jimmy Cliff . . . the *only* song played at Jerry's memorial service, and his favorite song, I think.

"If that's not a sign he was around me, I don't know what would be!"

Jeannie and Dorothy
(reprinted with author permission from a Facebook posting)
"Yesterday, the most amazing thing I've ever experienced took place at my aunt and uncle's house in Virginia. (Lily and I were there this past weekend for my grandma's Celebration of Life service.)

"For years my mom has told me that she asked her mom to send her a cardinal when she got to heaven. My aunt also asked her to send them a sign. They knew she would be in heaven but still desired a message from her. I believe this was because the three of them have been so incredibly close.

"Lily, my parents, my aunt, my uncle, and I were all sitting around the dining room table yesterday playing Canasta, my grandma's favorite card game. We heard a loud thud against the kitchen window. My aunt and uncle went out to investigate. My aunt came back in and said they didn't see anything. A couple of minutes later my uncle came in carrying a cardinal in his hands! He had hit the window and was sitting on the ground.

"Needless to say, we were all in complete awe. We all knew this had to be a sign from heaven above letting us know that my grandma was there, safe and happy. We had the cardinal inside for several minutes, all of us petting it. My mom and my aunt were both holding the cardinal. It was an incredibly emotional moment.

"After a few minutes we took the cardinal outside so he could fly away. My aunt was holding it, trying to encourage it to fly, but it kept holding on to her. My aunt placed the cardinal on my mom's shoulder. It sat there for a minute and then hopped down and sat right on her heart. For about eight minutes, they stood there holding the bird and the bird was holding onto them.

"They put the cardinal up on the branch. He sat there for a minute or so and then flew off. I cannot even begin to describe the way we felt. I know I will never experience anything like this ever again in my entire life. I was in the presence of a miracle.

"Just a few hours earlier, my mom and I had been talking about the cardinal sign she requested from her mother. She told me that she asked God to make it happen in such a way that she would have never thought of. In her mind, she would have seen a cardinal in California, because we do not get cardinals where we live. The Lord not only answered the prayer of my mom and my aunt, but He did it in such a way that there could be no doubt in anyone's mind that it was a sign from my grandmother to her sweet, caring, beloved daughters.

"The [Facebook] video is almost ten minutes [long] and starts after we went outside. It was very windy and cold but everyone wanted to stay and watch the cardinal fly away. And we did.

"Paul says in Ephesians 3, 'Now to Him who is able to do exceedingly abundantly above all that we ask or think, according to the power that works in us, to Him be glory in the church by Christ Jesus to all generations, forever and ever. Amen.'

"The Lord went so far and above the request of two of His precious daughters. He not only sent the sign, He literally put it in their hands. Exactly what they asked for but so much more. The Lord's kindness and goodness, His comfort, His peace, and His glory were surrounding us. There are no words."

(signed) Lori Wright Storey

(The video of this incredible experience was available on Facebook as I was writing this book, on February 15, 2019. But at the final edit of this book, in October 2021, I can't find it online anymore. I wish you could all watch as two older women try for a very long time to shoo away a wild bird that just won't go.)

(NOTE: re: the dream reports above: I know that psychiatrist Dr. Sigmund Freud might say that dream experiences are symbolic of the emotional state of the dreamer, and nothing more. But I believe that Dr. Carl Jung would feel that the same dreams can *also* contain messages from the spirit world.

As the dreamers reported on here believe to be so. And as I do.)

Chapter Twelve

Pets and Love

Shortly after I lost one of my beautiful cats, I received in the mail a poem by Elizabeth Frye. It had been sent to comfort me by the vet who had put the cat to sleep. The poem starts: "Do not stand at my grave and weep. I did not die. I do not sleep."

And it *was* a comfort, and it continues to be.

And so to love:

I can tell you right now that in major cities all over America, dogs and cats (and the occasional rabbit, gerbil, canary) are finding warm and caring homes with people who might feel isolated otherwise. Modern life can be stressful! And at a certain point in time, if you don't have a job and you're "too old" to go to bars and clubs, how do you meet people? I have to tell you that many I know don't even bother anymore. Instead, they're lavishing all their hearts on their pets. In return, they get unconditional love. A nice thing. (And there are so many people rescuing abused and abandoned animals these days, it makes my heart glad.)

But it also hurts like hell if you invest your whole heart in a little animal and that little animal passes away. It happened to me three times in my life. Over just a short period in the early 1990s, I lost Silly, Grey One, and Smasher, my own unconditional lovers for a lot of beautiful years.

When I set out to write this book, I decided to simply be a reporter. To try hard not to speculate about what could be. I decided I'd just tell you stories from my own life and the stories and information I could find from other places out there. This kind of rational approach seems especially important when it comes to the wrenching subject of the loss of animals and their survival into the afterlife.

So this section of this book may be short, but it's so very important.

PJ, my beautiful red dog, was the first loss. He went missing when I was divorcing my husband in the late 1970s. I'd had him since he was a puppy, and I had to leave him behind a few weeks until I was settled in the new place, forty miles away. PJ was always a happy dog: he cuddled kittens, he was a friend in need, he demanded almost nothing from me. I guess in his mind he was *my* dog (not ours), because I didn't realize that when I drove away that day he would try to follow. No, my ex didn't bother to tell me. As a result, about three weeks passed before I learned that PJ had disappeared that first day.

When I did find out that my dog hadn't been home in three weeks, I freaked. I feared the worst. And it killed me every day to even think about it. Anyway, I would never see him again.

Then, twenty years later, I decided out of the blue to go back to see the house I'd left that day. (I thought I was just going down a Western Massachusetts memory lane.) But for no reason, really, as I was leaving the house, I decided to stop in the next town over, park the car, and look around. I got out of the car and the first thing I saw? Across the street, well, I couldn't believe my eyes. There was a man on a basketball court playing fetch with a red dog with a white-tipped tail. Sure, it wasn't my dog. But for sure that animal came from him. There was no question in my mind. That white tail tip was just perfect, as was the rusty red color and the confused breed. And so, for the first time in twenty years, I was able not to think the worst about the fate of PJ. Somebody had found him and taken him in long, long ago! A hole was filled in my heart at that moment.

And two decades of awful guilt were erased, I might add.

Anyway, when I saw that man and his dog, I knew something. I realized that despite the reason I'd *thought* I was going back to that area, nothing in the "plan" accounted for me stopping and parking in that exact place on that exact hill in that strange town at that exact time. I'd been pulled there. I have no doubt. And now I could go home. As if it were mission accomplished after only sixty seconds, whatever that mission might really have been.

And then, as I turned to open the car door, a kind of low, dog-shaped shadow fell in beside me at my right side—I could almost *see* him—and I knew. I opened the car door wider, I took PJ into the car, and I drove back to Manhattan with him. He had waited for twenty (human) years, and finally I had come. Probably he's still here? I talk to him now as if he is.

Grey One, one of my three cats, died of cancer when she was about fourteen. A few days after she died, I saw her walking to the kitchen to the food dish, like a kind of hologram. It only happened once, but once was enough to tell me she'd come back.

Smasher, the black one of my three cats, died of cancer when she was about fifteen. That night, and for a few nights after, I could feel her padding across the bed at night. It was enough to tell me she'd come back. Then it stopped. I didn't know why, and I kind of missed feeling that before going to sleep! But a few years later, a psychic client came to me for a reading. I had to get up for some reason and she said, "Do you know there's a black cat following you around the apartment?"

No, I didn't know! But I was very glad. Smasher had told me she was here at the beginning, and then I guess she'd just settled in, at home once again.

I'd brought both Silly and Grey One from Massachusetts when I moved to Manhattan in 1975. Silly, the white one, died of cancer when she was about fifteen. And I waited for a sign for weeks, but I had no experience of her at all. No sounds, no images, no nothing. (I still never have.) But about six months after Silly died, I opened the fridge for something. And there, "dead"-center on the otherwise empty cover of the vegetable crisper, was a little piece of white cat fur about an inch square. An actual piece of fur, attached to skin that had hardened and blackened. A minor miracle, really, in the grand scheme of things. But this wouldn't be the last actual physical manifestation of a soul, a spirit, in my life.

Looking back, I see that this time was just going to be the first time.

Now what can I say? This stuff is impossible? This stuff doesn't happen? I'm crazy? Well, okay, maybe good questions—but none of the above.

See, it *isn't* impossible, it *does* happen, and those of us who have loved our pets totally have experiences with them all the time after they're gone. I'm not the only one.

So, listen: if you lose an animal you love, whether you can tell or not, they will at some point return to you in spirit.

Count on it.

It's a kind of endless love we humans have no clue yet how to achieve.

But I have hope.

Chapter Thirteen

Amedeo Modigliani Then . . .
and Now

This may be harder to write than I think. Well, I guess I'm about to find out.

Over the past six years, I've had a lot of time to think and to imagine and read. And what I think (so far) is that after we live here on Earth, we move into an Afterlife that can take three forms. First, some of us start to learn there. Second, some of us are assigned to watch over people who haven't yet passed away. Third, some of us are assigned to straddle both worlds in order to teach people who haven't yet passed away.

I believe the spirit of the man who came to my apartment six years ago and started this whole book ball rolling is in category three. And I believe his mission has been to create a teaching team with me, so that, as I learn, I share the lessons. This book is an example of that sharing. My conversations with people about all this are other examples of that sharing. And if I have any of this wrong, well, at least I've been thinking about it.

So, the teacher:

Fine artist Amedeo Clemente Modigliani was born in Livorno, Italy, on July 12, 1884. After a short lifetime struggling with tuberculosis, he died on January 24, 1920, in Paris, France. He was poor, but he was loved. Jeanne Hébuterne, an artist in her own right and his favorite model, became his partner in life and the mother of his daughter, Jeanne. When Modigliani became ill for the last time, it was Hébuterne who stayed with him through his final days. Two days after his death, she committed suicide when eight months pregnant with their second child.

It took me a while. But three years ago, I finally came to accept that Modigliani was the spirit who started coming to see me in 2016, the one I talk about earlier in this book.

But six years ago, when this all started happening, I thought it was Hébuterne who was visiting me in the middle of the night.

Then, two years later, I was telling medium Jeffrey Wands what had been happening in this apartment for so long. That she was visiting. He corrected me.

He said, "No. It's him."

Look, I was kind of shocked. "*Him*?" I mean, this is one of the greatest artists of the twentieth century. His paintings and sculptures sell for many millions of dollars. How would I ever *presume* to think he would come here, night after night? I mean, it never even *occurred* to me. (I'm a humble person, see. I don't "put on airs." Like they used to say on the radio a long time ago, "I'm just another bozo on the bus.")

So, hearing this from the medium I trust put a totally different spin on the story.

Not her. *Him*.

Here's what I told Jeffrey that day:

One night two years before, I awoke to "see" a kind of jittery painting "standing" somehow at the side of my bed. I recognized the style (a long-necked female) and the orangey color, as being Modigliani's work. Other than that, really, I had no idea about this man or his life. I'd never looked into it. Actually, I never really cared. My favorite painters at the time had been René Magritte and Edward Hopper. Not even close to the same style!

Anyway, I went back to sleep, figuring it was some kind of dream.

But in the morning, I awoke to find the long scarlet belt from my terry cloth robe had been arranged perfectly at the end of the bed. It was in the figure of a musical G clef. *What?*

The next night my sleep wasn't disturbed, but when I woke up there was the belt at the foot of my bed again. This time in the shape of an infinity symbol.

The third morning I awoke and found the belt in a *perfectly* straight line across the foot of the bed.

(My mother made this robe in the 1970s, and I've kept it all this time. I'd asked for a white robe. She made red. I have no idea why. And for many years, when it's cold outside, I've thrown the robe across the bed over the blanket. It works great as extra insulation.)

Anyway, now I realize I have some kind of thing going on in here. Somebody's coming here in the middle of the night, *removing the belt from the two loops,* and arranging it "artfully" at the foot of the bed.

But then, about a week after the straight line, I just "happened" to be on West 58th Street in Manhattan. I was coming back from a place I'd never been, and I was walking down this block I'd never been on. And there, in a gallery window, was the painting I'd seen that first night.

I was surprised and went closer. The little plaque on the frame said, "Jeanne Hébuterne." The painting was signed, "Modigliani."

That was when I'd started to assume (logically?) that it was this woman who'd begun coming to see me in the middle of the night.

At some point, though, I started to think twice. What could be going on? I went online and Googled "Modigliani red belt."

To my amazement, I found that this artist had in fact been obsessed with the long red sash from some piece of clothing. He'd wrap it around and around and around his waist, and then kind of unfurl himself by spinning like a top. (The story comes from Jean Cocteau, who found the spinning performance quite amusing.)

So now I was stunned. All of this was *connected* somehow? A painting, a belt, an artist, a model, a gallery window . . . me?

That was the moment when it struck me that maybe I had a lot to learn. In the 1970s, when it was fashionable, I'd read some books by people like Dr. Raymond Moody, Jr. and George Anderson. But after that, real life had taken over my thoughts and activities, and I put my curiosity about after-death on the back burner.

Now, though, I went out and bought two biographies of Modigliani and started reading. Well, I couldn't put them down. I *was* learning a lot of things about "Modi" (Dedo to his family). This included the bit that when he did all this red belt spinning around, he was drunk. But, look, when this guy was sober, you have to admit he was one heck of a painter.

Meanwhile. I was discovering that I *love* reading about the Paris of his day.

But when I was *in* Paris in 1977, on a tour bus in Montmarte and passing Sacré-Coeur Basilica, something started to "hurt" so much I couldn't bear it. I had to force the driver to let me off the bus, and I went straight to an Air France office and flew to London a few hours later. I remember this so clearly even now, but I also have no clue what was so upsetting that day. Yes, it was raining and gloomy. But something drove me clear out of France, and I have no idea why. I have to say here that among the things I've read about Modigliani and his friends, Sacré-Coeur, and Montmarte in general figure prominently. *Maybe* I'll know one day what all that was about. For now, I have to think some kind of emotional memory happened that dark afternoon on the bus.

Of course, there's so much more. Among the other things I've learned about "my" spirit artist is the fact that Modigliani went to séances. Interesting, right? As a matter of fact, around 1906 he painted two canvases: *Portrait of a Medium* and *Woman at a Séance*. So I have to think the artist was impressed enough by these supernatural events to sit down and devote time and talent to the subject of spirit communication.

And I've also learned this man was obsessed with being able to sculpt with marble. In particular, he dreamed of being able to sculpt in marble like the great Michelangelo.

Well, I just happen to have a strip of light grey marble with kind of a quiet pattern in it. This strip is raised and separates the bathroom floor from a little hallway floor. I had never taken a good look at it.

But one day, when I wasn't too far into reading the official biography, I noticed a hint of a face in that marble.

As I read on, over the days I could see that face "developing." When it finally stopped "developing," I found I was looking at a lovely, narrow-faced woman with a long neck. And décolletage. And a small cloche-type hat. She has a wistful smile. What else could I do? I traced it. And now I have a little picture on tissue paper I call "Modi in marble."

I also did this:

Early on, I went online again and found a photo of the artist's and Hébuterne's daughter, Jeanne, at age 64. I turned the computer screen to the room and said aloud, "See? Here's your little girl, all grown up." (I'd been reading that they both loved this kid.)

And then I went online and took a screen shot of Hébuterne. I printed and framed the little picture, and it's now on the wall and will stay there. Because, I figured, if my night visitor can see well enough to find the belt in the dark, or at least to feel the loops, take it off the robe, and use it to draw perfect figures with . . . then the photograph can be seen too, right? And appreciated?

Also, another word about this red belt: I now get the impression that "he" was pulling the belt from the loops by lifting it from the same central spot. Because the thing started wearing away right there, fraying in the middle for no reason. The effect of some kind of energy, I think. So, I took a picture before I repaired the spot the first time. Then the belt started fraying in a second central place, which is now also fixed. I didn't want the fabric to wear away. Because then there'd be just two small pieces of belt, and what would my visitor have to play with in the middle of the night? (I say this seriously.)

Anyway, this nightly visiting went on. For two years, almost every night.

Then, as time went by, as if he were aware that I'd made the connection between the man, Modigliani, and all these visits, my visitor was still removing the belt from the loops, but no more "drawings" were done with it. After that, it was always "just" loose on the bed or the floor when I woke up.

I have to tell you now that only a couple of people in my life are aware of this thing happening to me. I mean, I really don't need people thinking I'm nuts (or worse). So, I've shared it with only the few people I trust totally. Just two have seen the photo of the frayed belt and a photo of the tissue paper image in marble.

But now, of course, I'm announcing this thing to the world. What can I say? I guess it doesn't matter to me anymore what anybody thinks. I *know* this amazing thing has been happening to me for almost six years. And I'm pretty sure it's a miracle. So I've just decided to go with it.

Anyway, time passed and the visits were continuing, and then it was September 20, 2017. I'm sitting there with medium Jeffrey Wands in his little office in Port Washington and I'm telling him the story of how "she" has been coming every night for almost two years, meaning Hébuterne.

And that's when he corrects me, saying, "No. *He*."

And I'm saying, "What? It's not her?"

And he's saying, "No, it's him."

And I'm stunned.

And *then* Jeffrey's saying, "He's here."

"What??"

"He's here. And he's with Michelangelo and, I think, Manet."

I say, "What?"

But, by this point I'm also realizing that this medium has been accurate about everything else so far . . . still, *Michelangelo*?

"That can't be right," I say. (I'd read that true mediums see the people who lived in *our own* past lives.) "You mean, I knew *that* guy, too?"

Doubtful as I tend to be about my own past experiences, it did make me really happy to hear that the man was there with Modigliani. From my reading, I'd learned that my visitor had idolized Michelangelo in life. (As I said, he'd been desperate to sculpt in marble like his hero but had lungs too compromised by TB to be able to stand the dust.) It's just beautiful to think they're together in death.

Jeffrey says to my question about knowing both men, "You've had many lives." I think he had no idea at the time that the two were connected in any personal way, that Modigliani hero-worshiped Michelangelo. Because of this, I could believe a medium who had no clue. Because of this, I can be pretty sure the Renaissance genius and I lived at the same time. (As for Manet, I'm still on the lookout for a word of his relationship with Modigliani somewhere in recorded history. I can say, though, that the Renaissance genius, and Manet, and Modigliani are all considered "revolutionaries" in the art world. Maybe it's this contrary attitude that brought them together in the afterlife?)

I wish I could recall now, but I really don't remember what we said about these people after that, if anything. I do know I was really thrown for a loop. And who wouldn't be, right?

I also remember this: I told Jeffrey that my book on tarot (a mix of mysticism, physics, psychology, and my own "system") was to be published early in 2019. Then I added, "But what I'd really like is my novels published. Do you see that?"

And Jeffrey said, "You'll publish many books. But *they* (and he gestured around the room behind me) want you to do more like this [the tarot book]."

Yes, it was kind of a vague supposed "request" from a bunch of spirits, but I did understand suddenly. Maybe I do have something to share? Well at least "they" thought so? At hearing this, I figured that maybe I should at least think about it . . . when I came back to planet Earth, that is. As I said, visiting a true medium can be beyond uplifting.

Still, I replied, "Well, I have no idea what I'd write about."

I remember Jeffrey shrugging.

And again, we moved on to other things.

Nine months passed. Then it was June 2018. The belt was still coming out of the loops a few times a week.

And I suddenly knew that what I could write about, in detail, is all the stuff in this book. People say, "Write about what you know." Well, what I know from my life experience is here in this book, but what I've learned from research is also here.

I started writing.

And here's something that made me sad. But I thought it also totally *affirmed* everything I just told you. When I started writing, I thought Modigliani stopped coming. I mean, no more belt tricks? I mean, you have to understand that at some point I started feeling a kind of kinship with the guy. I still don't know if I knew him in his lifetime. And if so, how we were related. But I do seem to feel something, some kind of real emotion, having read the bios and thought about him and his life and having had this experience for so long.

Not to mention that I finally *accepted* that here I sit in the midst of something miraculous. And all wrought by his spirit. In fact, I felt so close to him that at one point I went to the Jewish Museum. They were showing a traveling exhibit of his drawings. I invited Modigliani to come along. (Just in case he could.)

Well, anyway, I was there maybe five minutes when I could kind of sense him over my right shoulder. This was a whole new thing, this sensation stuff. And I felt he was angry, looking at a particular drawing. And somehow, I felt he was angry and thinking, "I could've done better."

At the end of this particular exhibit, there was also a death mask of him made by fellow artists. I wondered how he might feel if he could see that. I'll never know. But when I left, I was the one crying. And I have no idea why.

I have to say here, too: During all this, twice in three years I'd gone to Florida for several months at a time. And nothing had happened there at all. Back here, I'd left the robe on the couch in a particular shape, with the belt prominent. When I got home, I found that nothing had been disturbed.

Anyway, now it seems you're all reading a book I was urged to write by a bunch of spirits . . .

And you know what else? Something about this whole thing feels totally right. When Jeffrey mentioned writing another mystical book, I couldn't imagine it.

But now . . .

Well, now all I can think is that maybe (as I said) Modigliani and I have a mission *together*. Maybe at some point, long ago, he'd decided he'd bug me in the 21st century until I wrote *his* message to the world. And I had agreed I would do it. And then we'd be done. (Or not?)

Of course, I'll never know about that. But it's okay. As I said, the idea just *feels* totally right.

And about that G clef? The very first "picture" he "drew" years ago with the red belt? Well, it was only two months ago that I realized what the heck he was trying to tell me. *Music!* Specifically, I think he was trying to point me to the movie song about the great composer, Mozart: "Amadeus, Amadeus." He was not only trying to "show" me his painting, but also trying to sign his name at the foot of my bed. What more does one need?

Okay . . . so sometimes I don't catch on too quick. This all took quite a while in Earth time. And, still, I didn't get there on my own!

Thank you, Dedo.

* * *

It turns out, though, he hadn't left at all.

For some reason, after I finished what I just wrote about the man, the spirit, and his visits here, the belt started migrating around again. Other things started happening, too. A large spool of yellow embroidery thread was removed from the bookcase and placed on the floor right below where it had been. Little things a friend had given me were moved around on the dresser one night. Another time, a very old little alarm clock had been laid on its side in the middle of the night. Stuff like that.

One amazing time, I awoke to find a piece of drawstring from pajamas had been laced through my hair. I'd been wearing the PJs the night before . . . *under* a sheet and a blanket and the red robe . . . and I'd given up trying to un-knot the string . . .

So, I have to wonder if Dedo was getting bored and was now maybe doing variations on a theme? Well, I don't know. But coming home to my apartment every day was starting to be like a magical mystery tour! And still is.

And, you know, I've stopped feeling sad. I do think he was telling me something by disappearing for a few days. I assumed at first the reason was that our mission was accomplished (whatever that is). But now I think he's trying to tell me something else by leaving and coming back.

Maybe we have more to do "together"? And maybe he has somewhere else to go *between visits* to me? Is he being taught, too? Is there another "student" somewhere?

* * *

At long last, I've now written this book. But it seems that Modigliani isn't done with me!

About six months after I finished the first draft of the book, ending with the last chapter, I found a piece of yellow yarn on the floor. Yes, I have such yarn. It's in a ball in a closed bag in a closed closet. But there it was. On the floor.

I left it there and had to kind of jump around it to get to the kitchen. LOL.

Then, after maybe a couple of weeks, I "happened" to notice my old red tee-shirt was falling apart. I tore a strip from it, without a plan, and replaced the yellow yarn on the floor with the red "string." I figured if he'd chosen that spot to do something new, I should use the same spot.

Well, the night I laid that red string on the floor in a straight line was the night the floodgates opened!

Every morning was a new design there on the floor. (I have so many photos of these. If you go to theafterlifebook.com, you'll find all the photos.)

But then the designs started coming *while I was awake and in the same room.* A couple of times, I went to the desk for a second or two, turned around, and, voila, there was *another* design, *two inches* from my feet. All I can think is that at first he hadn't wanted to scare me and did things only when I wasn't here or awake. But when I wasn't scared, it freed him to do stuff whenever, night or day.

Then, something even more amazing happened.

As I said, I'd been reading biographies of Modigliani and learning things about him and his society and the people who mattered to him.

So, one day I asked *in my mind* if he could give me a clue as to when we *might* have known each other in another life. The next morning, I awoke and found a red "S" on the floor. The morning after that, it was a "V."

This is beyond beautiful. See, in one of the bios there's a story: Modigliani's "surrogate mother" in Paris was the mother of his friend, the painter Maurice Utrillo. She was a fine painter in her own right who accepted Modigliani warts and all. Her name was Suzanne Valadon. It is said that toward the end of his young life and fearing death, he found her and her husband at a cafe, sat close to her, put his head on her shoulder and wept. Well, that is so damned sad.

So then I got a bio of this woman. I learned: Both of us wanted to join the circus. Both of us wanted to work the trapeze. Both of us love flower images (she painted them, I photograph). She succeeded in going up on a trapeze, then had a bad accident and crushed her hip. And I have wondered all my life why I was born with scars on my hip. . .

At some point I'll go back to Jeffrey Wands and ask directly if I was Valadon.

"S V."

(As you can see from the pics in this book, the letters are clear and unquestionable.)

Meanwhile, though, what do I think is *the most important* part of the story? I asked for a clue, *and I got one.* Not in my mind. *For real,* on the floor. We were *talking, communicating back and forth,* and it wasn't (and isn't still) just a mental exercise on my part. No "channeling" here. This is what scientists *look* for: *physical proof!*

Then there is the episode of the seagull. At one point, I said *in my mind* that it must be easy to paint a seagull in flight. Next morning? The red string was now a seagull in flight, no question.

Then there was something even more amazing.

It was a hot summer last year. I was undressed, taking a nap on the couch. Suddenly, a small couch cushion lightly hit my arm after traveling maybe two feet across the couch. It woke me up. And that's when I could hear the machinery of a scaffold approaching the window. I had just enough time to cover up before the two workers showed up outside.

Amedeo, my new protector.

Then it was November. A few days before the 8th, I found a wooden coffee stirrer on my floor. Slightly bowed. Never used (no coffee stains). Three days later, I broke a bone in my hand. A cast was put on. And thanks to that little bowed stirrer, I was able to scratch under the cast. It, too, had the *exact same* bow shape.

So, twice that I knew of, he'd *anticipated* my needs when I myself was clueless.

But then there was this: I thought I was doing just fine dealing with the COVID pandemic. Until I learned very recently that I clench my jaws at night and grind my teeth and have been basically doing a bad number on my mouth. My dentist suggested, "Maybe you should try meditation or yoga?" And holy smoke, it hit me: A few months *before* (maybe when this jaw thing started?), my protector made an unusual design, a surprisingly complicated design, that I felt at first sight looked like the lotus position. The next night, clueless me was treated to a bit of an alteration of the design, still a yoga pose but different. Did I think about it twice? Nope. But now I look back and I see that once again my painter was trying to warn me about something serious, and I wouldn't realize it for three more months.

This is not to mention the little gifts: Like the quarter that fell into my lap one day as I was eating dinner. It seemed to come from under the table. Like the piece of yellow quartz that appeared one day under the instep of my bare foot, as I worked at my computer, and "predicted" something that happened soon after. I have no idea how he does this. I only know it happens. Research tells me that such things, things that just appear, are called *apports*. Okay then.

(By the way, I offered to pay for a polygraph about all this stuff, to "prove" to my publisher that none of it is my doing and all of it is true, but my publisher has decided to believe in me and my work here. Thank you, Skyhorse.)

So now, Modigliani continues to come and go. Or maybe he's always here? For sure, he's hearing me, wherever he is. Sometimes he disturbs the red string just enough that I know it's "hello." Or he makes an undulating line, like a *wave*. Other times, he makes images. A few months ago, I added a piece of orange yarn and a piece of forest green, to see what would happen. Then a piece of white floss. He's now using them all at one time or another. Sometimes he moves two or three together so they touch. I'm sure it is his intelligence trying to tell me something. So far, though, the messages are eluding me.

Anyway, by this point, after almost six years of "togetherness," I have to believe that this artist and I knew each other in the past. And I believe that we agreed to meet in the future, now, *as a team*. I believe our purpose is to teach the world something. I take no credit for any of this. Actually, sometimes it just feels more like what I'm taking is dictation. LOL.

And when I think he's disappeared for good, and for a few days there are no "messages," again I tend to feel sad. But I kind of also know he'll be back. I now consider Amedeo Modigliani *"mon ami,"* my friend.

And you know what? Throughout a year of COVID isolation, I'm *certain* I haven't been alone. I'm not alone. I've never *felt* alone. I talk to Dedo a lot in French, as if he's in the room. Out loud and in my head. I show him things (*voila*! the Moon, a star, the Sun). Once, I played Itzhak Perlman (on YouTube) because I read that he used to paint at night while Hébuterne played the violin. I think he liked it. Me? I started crying.

Go figure.

And then this happened: *years* after that first G clef, I was looking around YouTube and happened to see the icon for the musical, "Amadeus." I pointed it out to my friend. A few minutes later, I got up from the computer and that little yellow piece of yarn was now on the carpet in the shape of . . . a G clef. "Yes," he was saying, "you had it right back then. I was trying to tell you who I was." Meanwhile, this symbol on the carpet has moved me back to music in earnest, every day. I hope he can hear it too.

* * *

By the way, it took me many days to feel comfortable addressing this man. What name should I use? How should I speak to him? Finally, I settled on "Dedo," because it just feels right. He and his family used that pet name for him all his life. Now? Now I know I'd be uncomfortable calling him anything else.

* * *

Long ago, Pythagoras and other ancient Greek philosophers believed that *personality* persists after death. These days, among others, Deepak Chopra does too.

Well, what I can add to that is *intelligence*. From personal experience, I know that the spirit in my life is also smart and a mind-reader and an able communicator (with enormous physical powers). At one point, this guy (who was known for his practical jokes) changed one of his own designs to the straight line I was always creating, which was *my* "job." Well, I saw that, and I got the joke, and I laughed like hell. He has thoughts, and he communicates them clearly.

Bottom line? Yes, I can tell the ancients: personality and intelligence do persist after death.

And another thing I'm sure of: *heart* persists too.

This spirit worries I'll be embarrassed if building workers see me undressed, and he warns me. He knows I'm going to be spending six uncomfortable weeks in a cast and provides a scratcher. He weaves a piece of string through my hair, and I know it's meant as a gentle gift.

And those are heartfelt things.

At this point there's only one question I would ask my friend. Does everything happen for him at the same time? Weeks go by for me, and for him it's all kind of simultaneous?

I hope someday he'll tell me.

Finally, *this* happened, the single most amazing thing of all. It occurred to me one day to wonder if my friend's *artistic genius* exists for him in the afterlife. I wondered about it because, outside of what I thought were the lotus position and a seagull, there had been no actual pictures.

Two days later, after this crossed my mind, I found a long thin chain on the floor in a puddle. (The chain had been somewhere in my closet.) I dutifully straightened it into a line.

Two days later, that chain was a *perfect picture of a bird*. I will *never* disturb this drawing on purpose. It's protected by a door . . . and I hope it will stay that way. A great artist who died in 1920 has put on my floor *101 years later* a totally clear drawing of a bird . . . with a heart in its beak. (The photo is here in the book.) I call it just *"L'Oiseau"* . . . "bird." It's only slightly stylized, and it made me think of Egyptian hieroglyphics. I looked up the meaning of the Egyptian bird motif. It means *soul*.

Once again, Dedo has read my mind and replied to an *un*asked question with a perfectly clear answer. I stand in awe.

Chapter Fourteen

Dreams and Hypnosis

Dreams

On December 28, 2004, Jerry Orbach died. He was the fabulous actor who brought Lenny Briscoe to life every week for years on *Law & Order*. To be clear, I didn't know this man. We'd never communicated in any way. We'd never even met in passing. I just really admired Lenny's shambling walk and edgy attitude, not to mention his character flaws and a heart as big as Texas. All of which the actor portrayed to perfection.

The night after he passed away, there he was, this stranger really, in my sleep. It was like a vivid, still photograph I was looking at. A flash, in color, that I remember even today, eighteen years later. The actor was standing in a doorway, grinning at me. He was leaning against the doorjamb in a quite jaunty way. He was wearing brown slacks and a short-sleeved, light-colored shirt.

Now I have to explain something. I learned a long time ago that I have two kinds of dreams. One is normal dreaming and looks like movie film. The other is psychic and looks like what you see when something's being videotaped. (I've read that other people report the same dreaming styles.)

Anyway, this image of Mr. Orbach that night had the visual quality of the taped kind of dream. Which means that I knew when I awoke it had been a psychic dream. For some weird reason, this man had stopped off to see me on his way away? Or maybe, as has happened before a couple of times . . . maybe in my dream state I'd mentally "connected" with the *intended* recipient of his visit?

This isn't so far-fetched. For me, anyway. For example: one night long ago, I dreamed that two little boys were in the street, and one was killed by a truck. In the dream, I saw a black-and-white picture of the scene. The next afternoon, my therapist tried mightily to understand with me what it could all mean. We got nowhere. But the morning after that, there it was. The *very same* black-and-white photo on the front page of the paper, along with a story about the two little brothers and the accident and the death.

So much for trying to psychoanalyze some of my dreams!

And so I am able to imagine that maybe I did manage to get my "wires crossed" again. Maybe it was with Mrs. Orbach or somebody else close to him. But I saw him. Well, if that's the case, I hope the other person was able to see him too. These goodbye visits are so important to those left behind. (There's also the possibility that for a time I was "connected" to somebody who was reading a particular newspaper every morning, or to a worker at that paper. This idea first crossed my mind when dreams like the truck dream started to happen a lot.)

Now I need to talk a little bit here about the human brain.

It's divided into two physical sections (hemispheres). In street language, we're talking here about the right brain and the left brain. The left brain makes sense of things, adds numbers, spells, memorizes. Stuff like that. The right brain imagines things and creates art. And when we're asleep, I think it's the right brain that dreams.

That's kind of a simple explanation.

Anyway, what I've discovered over the years is that when I do psychic work, my left brain turns off pretty much. I'm not thinking. Mostly I'm doing.

Look at it this way:

To learn to drive a car, you memorize the rules of the road. You learn to manage the vehicle and learn what everything in it is for. And then you think about every move you're making as you drive. Well, all that work is being done by the left brain.

Then one fine day, you suddenly realize you've been driving along and *not once* has it occurred to you to *think* about what you're doing. And you realize that you've been on kind of automatic pilot, reacting to things without even having to think about it. Well, of course, all that time your left brain was still alive and kicking. It just wasn't really paying attention. I mean, maybe you're driving along and imagining date night. That, for sure, is right brain all the way!

I think the same thing happens when we sleep. The left brain is subdued for a while and gets to rest after all the hard work it's done all day long. While the right brain takes over and imagines things. When we're awake, this purely right brain activity can lead to art. When we're asleep, it can lead to dreams.

So then, while I was asleep on December 29, 2004, my left brain was "off." I was dreaming. No conscious thinking was interfering with my "connection" to Jerry Orbach. And, look, it was such a vivid image! As I said, it's still with me, even all these years later.

Now back to the point:

Think about it. How many times have you heard stories about spirits visiting people in their sleep? Coming to them in the form of dreams? A lot, right?

Well, too many of us dismiss that stuff. We say, oh, it was *just* a dream. Well, no, maybe it *wasn't* just a dream. But the person who was left behind is thinking so much all day long, the only way for the departed loved one to get through is to show up during sleep.

This happened to me only twice. The first time, I dreamed that the man I loved was on a "silver river out of Corpus Christi" and coming "home." Well, I've never been to Texas, and I've never seen such a river. But then I learned that the night of the dream was the night he died, in the Southwest, a long way from home.

On this subject of spirits and dreaming, I've found an explanation that's so clear I'm repeating it all here. Amanda Linette Meder writes online:

". . . in our dreams, when we are most aware of our inner land-scape, we happen to also be *least resistant* to messages from Spirit People." She says that if we feel little touches on our bodies when we're awake, we might ignore them. When in fact this is a spirit trying hard to speak and we're just not listening.

She goes on to say that sometimes we get a feeling to reach out to somebody right away, but we don't, and again we may have ignored a spirit trying to tell us something. "Often," she tells us, "their nudges come from within, using our energy to connect with us. Speaking can be difficult without a voice box of your own, after all."

"For each one of us," she explains, "the space without an opportunity for dismissal is in unconscious sleep."

So there it is. We hear things, we see things, and we choose to decide they're nothing. When we're awake.

But when we're sleeping, there's no choosing and no deciding.

That means, whether you're asleep or awake, please pay attention from now on. Somebody may be trying to get through to you, to connect with you. One of my friends has had a cardinal show up in her life. I've had feathers. And I told you about me and the insects and the birds. And I'm so damned grateful that I know what it is: it's people who still love me saying "goodbye" AND "hello."

Think about it. How much of value have you been throwing away by thinking and deciding and analyzing. Why not just accept that what you're throwing away as meaningless may really be important, and possible?

Look, it can't hurt, right?

Hypnosis
"Hypnosis is the oldest Western form of psychotherapy, but it's been tarred with the brush of dangling watches and purple capes," says Dr. David Spiegel. The speaker holds the Jack, Samuel and Lulu Willson Professorship in Medicine at Stanford University School of Medicine. "In fact," he goes on, "it's a very powerful means of changing the way we use our minds to control perception and our bodies."

And from the website, howstuffworks.com, we learn this: It's been discovered that when we're hypnotized there is reduced activity in the left hemisphere of the brain, while activity in the right hemisphere often increases. Scientists believe that the left hemisphere deals with logic and reasoning. The right hemisphere, on the other hand, is the source of creativity. This means that when we see less activity in the left hemisphere during hypnosis, an increase in right-brain activity shows the creative mind taking charge.

Long story short? Hypnosis kind of puts the left brain to sleep, which means the right brain can take over and imagine without limits.

Just as with dreams and the dream state, the person who is hypnotized is set free to imagine, without self-censorship. In a funny way, little kids do this all the time. But as we mature, we lose that freedom to just *be* . . . and that's just sad.

I once saw a *60 Minutes* episode that was fascinating. They hypnotized a bunch of advanced students. (If I remember correctly, some were musicians, others were painters.) They were told they could create art as great as the artists they admired. And you know what? They were doing it. They had the technique, they'd been at it for years, they had a passion for their art, and they had left brains that just kind of stepped away a while. They didn't think they *couldn't* do it . . . and so they could!

Then there's the British psychotherapist who hypnotizes himself for surgery because he doesn't do well with anesthetics. According to a (London) *Telegraph* story about psychotherapist Alex Lenkei:

"A British man who hypnotized himself before surgery last week so he could skip the anesthetic says he was fully awake and pain-free during the 83-minute procedure." (I won't give you the details of the surgery, but it sounds to me as if it was brutal.)

Lenkei himself said, ". . . there's a lesson to be learned here for the medical profession, 'basically, that hypnosis can be actually used post- and pre-operation to actually help the patient (relax) for a much better, successful operation. And I feel that doctors ought to investigate this in a lot more detail and actually use it for the benefit of the patient.'"

(I remember my own very enlightened dentist experimenting with hypnosis back in the 1970s. No, I admit I never had the guts to try it. I mean, hey, trying something like that at the *dentist*?)

There's also this: I quit smoking in 1985. Four friends did as well. They were hypnotized . . . and so they expected to stop wanting a cigarette. But it didn't work out that way. All four of them were all back to smoking within months. I managed to stay off nicotine *because*

I fought like crazy every day for 366 days until I stopped wanting/needing/obsessing over cigarettes.

From these things, I'm guessing that addiction isn't something all of us can tackle and overcome with hypnosis. *Determination* and *will* are how we beat our devils into submission (left brain all the way).

So, then, I knew all this when I visited the psychotherapist in the late 1990s for my hypnotic regression. If it worked, I knew that my very active and intrusive and critical and doubting and questioning left brain would be calmed for a while. And if that happened, at least I might be able to dream up a novel or a play or something with my right brain.

But that didn't happen.

What did happen was kind of time travel, as I said, back at least 23,000 years . . . which might be ridiculous when you think about it. Unless you're me and just love having had the experience.

As I mentioned earlier, I transcribed the one-and-a-half-hour regression when the Internet showed up on my desk. I wanted to check things out. I am SO left-brained And I was glad to see confirmation of things I don't think I'd ever read or been taught.

As for reaching the spirit world via hypnosis: according to the Afterlife Research Institute online: We can all be receptive to the messages of loved ones. All we have to do is *allow* them to come through. Usually, we're just too busy to be able to just be still and let them come, but under hypnosis we have the ability to connect and receive the unspoken messages of others.

Dr. Brian Weiss, "Catherine," and Hypnosis

I want to praise Dr. Weiss here, first of all, for his courage. He is an eminent psychiatrist and brain researcher with impeccable credentials. I believe that, like Carl Jung, he literally risked his career and the respect of his colleagues to write the book *Many Lives, Many Masters*. In this book Weiss chronicles the hypnotic regression memories of a young woman he named "Catherine."

This is an astonishing story not only for the detail of the lives she was able to remember and the richness of her memories, but also for the fact that Weiss (like me) refused to accept anything on faith. He's a scientist who looks for real-time, earthly ways to prove things, to substantiate things. So, it wasn't until "Catherine" started giving him detailed information about his own life and family and family history that he started to realize *this* was the real deal. (Dr. Weiss wants us to understand that, at first, no way he believed in the world "Catherine" was opening up to him. Now he does.)

As a result of his experiences with "Catherine," Dr. Weiss started doing his own research. Along the way, he found Dr. Ian Stevenson (as I did) and the many others who'd been laboring in the psychic fields for a long time, ignored and rarely respected.

As for his patient, "Catherine" wasn't an academic. She worked in an ordinary job and lived an ordinary life . . . when she was awake. But in the deep sleep of hypnosis? Well, that was a totally different ball game.

Dr. Weiss writes that he came to understand there was a purpose for "Catherine" seeking *him* out in the first place. He realized that this had as much to do with him as it did with helping her deal with her psychological issues. He was right. *Together* they made quite a team. "Together" they produced an amazing book. Under hypnosis, "Catherine" called him her "teacher." But it's clear from *Many Lives, Many Masters* that she was just as much teacher to him.

Then the time came, Dr. Weiss tells us, that once "Catherine's" psychological issues were resolved, there was no more need for her to see him. No more need for hypnosis. He describes the formerly fearful and conflicted young woman as having become radiant and beautiful. He says she had a kind of energy that people were being attracted to. And he tells us that this included some of the same people who hadn't even noticed her before the regression experience!

I wish that a lot more credible research would be done into this hypnosis-spirit communication thing. I'm hoping that, as time goes on, more and more people will become receptive to the idea that communication like this is possible. If that could happen, then more and more serious people could become interested in investigating it. There *are* times when the left brain is needed, and this would be one of them . . . *science* looking at spirit.

But the bottom line for now?

Right brain = the potential for spirit communication.

Left brain = the near certainty that we'll dismiss or ignore anything that "doesn't make sense."

And ignoring all this is a damn shame. Because all that "nonsensical" stuff can be so beautiful and helpful and uplifting, you know?

Been there, done that.

I do know.

Chapter Fifteen

The Times They Are a'Changin

I didn't know how I was going to finish this book. (Heck, I didn't even know how I was going to start it!) And as I went along, I still didn't know what I'd want to say. Finally, though, I decided just to take off my reporter hat and my storyteller hat and simply talk a little here about what I think.

Between 1959 and 1964, American television aired a series with such powerful messages that it has stood the test of time. It's still in reruns on cable stations. This was the brilliant Rod Serling's *The Twilight Zone*, which set out to turn the world on its head. We're "asked" to watch this show without preconceived notions. We're supposed to do it with what movie people call "suspension of disbelief."

I see the content of this series as meant occasionally to startle, sometimes to educate, but always to jar us from any kind of complacency about the world we think we live in.

I'm talking about *The Twilight Zone* here because one episode that I'll never forget totally makes the point I want to make. "Eye of the Beholder" deals with a woman so deformed she can't blend in with her society. The woman's face is heavily bandaged throughout the episode. We see and hear the doctors and nurses and others only as voices and as shadows on the wall. This is how it is until the last minute. When the bandages come off and the lights come on, we find that the woman is actually beautiful (by *our* standards). And we're shocked to realize that the *medical staffers* are the monstrous-looking ones (by *our* standards).

This is powerful and thought-provoking. But what in the world has it got to do with spirits?

Well, this episode of a major TV show teaches us that we tend to understand, expect, and accept what we're *taught* to understand, expect, and accept. In a world of monstrous-looking people, beauty is seen as deformity. And the people of that world learn to accept this as true. In fact, it's kind of like a rule in that world. And so, the episode is teaching us what it means to be biased.

After I wrote these lines, I came across a wonderful book by scientist Rupert Sheldrake. In his *Science and Spiritual Practices*, he says, "In traditional hunter-gatherer societies, there was no distinction between religion and the rest of social and cultural life. The existence of spirits, the invisible influence of ancestors . . . were taken as a given."

Then, he tells us, came the overwhelming influence of organized religion and of what we call "science."

And so in our world, we learn to doubt the presence of spirit life, because we haven't been *raised* to understand, expect, and accept that it's a "normal" part of the life cycle. Which means that mainstream society has always looked at spiritualism as kind of an abnormal "deformity" in a modern world designed by and dictated by science and "common sense."

And Carl Becker, in his wonderful book, *Paranormal Experience and Survival of Death*, puts this in historical context. He says, "At least as long ago as the Neanderthal, human beings have expected there to be some kind of life after death. The ancient literature of the world is filled with accounts of people meeting the ghosts of their ancestors, leaving their bodies, or visiting the next world on their death beds. But the materialism, the cynicism, and 'scientism' of the modern West have tended to treat life after death as just so much nonsense or superstition."

Mr. Becker wrote those words twenty-six years ago.

But something else, something new, seems to be happening now. Somewhere in the past twenty years, it looks as if the spirits may be getting the better of us at last (thank goodness!). I see now that our *refusal* to understand and accept is slowly being worn away.

At least, that's what I *think* is happening, though I have no idea why. Why now?

Think about it: Say you're born into a world where nobody says psychic and spirit phenomena are impossible. Say that in that world nobody ever tells you that you're governed only by physical things. Well, in that world, how much trouble would you have believing in things you can't see, feel, taste, touch, smell? Like our prehistoric ancestors, you'd be right there, along for the ghostly ride, right?

I mean, if we were taught from day one that invisible things that can't be proved *can still be real*, most of us wouldn't think twice about accepting them.

My point here is simple. I don't think it's just human nature to deny the existence of an afterlife populated by the continued existence of us. What I think is that we've *learned* a whole damn wrong thing.

You've heard the riddle, "If a tree falls in the forest, does it make a sound?" If there are no ears to *hear* sound, is there sound? Well, science tells us that the impact of the tree hitting the ground would generate sound waves. (Then again, I didn't hear a thing when the maple tree almost killed me after being struck by lightning. As I said, I remember only the little tickling of the topmost little branch down my back at the end.)

And how do we know there's carbon monoxide? I mean, we can't see it and we can't smell it, but it can still kill us. Well, we know it's there because we're *taught* that it's there. Because science knows how carbon monoxide is created, and there are machines that can detect it. From all of this comes the idea that we can believe the gas can exist and never see it coming.

But now, here's a different idea.

Say I have a child. And my child tells me he sees dead people. Well, I have two choices. I can choose to believe my kid. Or I can choose not to believe my kid. There's no in-between.

So far, too many of us just reject what such a kid says as fantasy or daydreaming. We do this either because we don't believe in life after death; or we do believe in an afterlife but not that it's populated; or we don't believe any kind of dead being would be communicating with *our* kid . . . So, we don't even bother to listen to the child. We just dismiss the whole thing. (Now you should be asking yourself just how many kids' "imaginary friends" are all that imaginary, right?)

And then there's the other, equally terrible thing. It's what happened to the woman in eastern Massachusetts, who could hear music in the walls of her apartment. She was *institutionalized* for it, probably until she "came to her senses" and was "smart" enough to deny the whole thing. OMG. And she hasn't been the only one locked away for being aware of what society today refuses to acknowledge.

I want to explain here that it took me many years to *unlearn* all the so-called "rules" about how our world works. It took me, a scientist at heart, a long time to realize that science actually has limits. That our senses aren't perfect. And that many great and respected thinkers have come to the same conclusions.

But for sure, none of this spiritual stuff is anything we're going to learn in school any time soon. And definitely not in Sunday school. And maybe not even from Hollywood.

Actually, it looks to me as if current tribal cultures, as "backward" as we may think they are . . . well, these cultures may actually be *light-years ahead* of the rest of us. At least when it comes to their awareness of spirit life and the back-and-forth communication that's possible between us and spirits.

Carolyn Myss takes this one step farther when she talks about Native American Spirituality at myss.com. The belief, she says, " . . . known as animism, is common to many preliterate religions which hold that personal, intelligent spirits inhabit almost all natural objects, from stones, plants, and rivers to insects, birds, animals, trees, and mountains, but [don't hold that] all places [are] sacred." She says, "Certain locations and animals are singled out as manifestations of the supernatural, including those seen in dreams and visions."

Myss likens this idea to the ancient concept of *kami* in the Shinto tradition of Japan. In this tradition, "Animals, places, even stones and trees can possess spirits that interact with humans in a kind of cosmic harmony . . ."

What this says to me is that *pre*-industrial (*pre*-"scientific") civilizations can be far more in touch with the world of spirits than we can. *They can be far more in touch with their own invisible natures than we can.* For them, it's simply a matter of culture and teaching. I mean, if we were learning animism in elementary school, it would never occur to us to question if there's a spirit in a pebble. See?

To put it a different way: In the world of moving street vehicles, green means go and red means stop. That's what we learn until it's instilled in our bones. But we could be taught just the opposite, right? And *as long as we all believed the same thing*, then we'd all be fine on the road.

So, this is about the *idea language* we're taught to speak. (This communication and word choice thing is a very big deal in the card game of bridge. One of the major keys to winning is to "communicate" well with your partner. And it really doesn't matter what "language" you use, as long as you're both on the same page about bidding.)

Then, what I think is simple, and it boils down to this: Something is happening these days to *re-educate* us. Something is happening to encourage us to throw away ideas that might not be true, and to at least think about ideas that might be. And as Myss tells us, looking back to primal nature and primal times may be just the way to discover what might be true.

You see, there *is* a spirit living in my apartment. He does little things, he moves things around, he plays with my clothing. I didn't invent him. Maybe he invented me? Who knows? (I mean, it took a medium just to tell me it's a *he*.)

But I do know one thing. From my spirit story search among strangers, I find that I'm not the only one with the hands-on spirit experience. And I'm guessing that many of you others out there are starved for an outlet. You wish that you, too, could just *tell somebody* and not be ridiculed or rejected . . . or committed to an institution until you dropped the whole thing and just plain went along.

And it's a good thing that society seems to be changing about this, right? Sure, the change is slow, but at least I believe it's happening . . . finally.

W. H. Church tells us: "Superstitions we call them. Yet the educated skepticism of our modern age in the face of unseen forces in our midst may not be so much a sign of our intellectual achievement as a symptom of our waning spiritual awareness under the rapid onslaught of materialism."

I hope all the ignorance will be gone soon. And that a little bit of enlightenment can be coming now.

I mean, the fact that this book has been published, and you can be reading it today, is all the proof I need! Values are changing. Minds are changing.

Change is in the wind.

References and Reading List

Chapter 1

Deepak Chopra, *Life After Death: The Burden of Proof.* New York: Harmony Books, 2006.

The Journal of Religion and Psychical Research

Rhine Education Center (in-person and online course work)

https://smithsonian.com

Harry Houdini, *A Magician Among the Spirits.* Ayer Co., 1972.

Doris Kearns Goodwin, *Team of Rivals: The Political Genius of Abraham Lincoln.* New York: Simon & Schuster, 2006.

Ernest B. Furguson, *Freedom Rising: Washington in the Civil War.* New York: Vintage, 2005.

Adam Selzer, *Ghosts of Lincoln: Discovering His Paranormal Legacy.* Woodbury: Llewellyn Publications, 2015.

firstladies.org

Sam Roberts, *Grand Central: How a Train Station Transformed America.* New York: Grand Central Publishing, 2017.

Elise Gainer, *Ghosts and Murders of Manhattan.* Mount Pleasant: Arcadia Publishing, 2015.

Chapter 2

Michio Kaku, *The God Equation: The Quest for a Theory of Everything.* New York: HarperOne, 2021.

Zhi Gang Sha and Rulin Xiu. *Tao Science: The Science, Wisdom, and Practice of Creation and Grand Unification.* Heaven's Library Publication Corp., 2017.

Carlo Rovelli, *Helgoland: Making Sense of the Quantum Revolution.* Milan: Adelphi Edizioni, 2020.

Alice Calaprice, *Dear Professor Einstein: Albert Einstein's Letters to and from Children.* Buffalo: Prometheus, 2002.

https://www.nationalgeographic.com

George Greenstein, *Quantum Strangeness: Wrestling with Bell's Theorem and the Ultimate Nature of Reality.* Cambridge: MIT Press, 2019.

Russell Targ, *Limitless Mind: A Guide to Remote Viewing and Transformation of Consciousness.* Novato: New World Library, 2004.

F. W. H. Myers, *Human Personality and the Survival of Bodily Death.* Mineola: Dover, 2005.

Ervin László, *Science and the Akashic Field: An Integral Theory of Everything.* Rochester: Inner Traditions, 2007.

Stephen Braude, *Immortal Remains: The Evidence for Life after Death.* Lanham: Rowman & Littlefield, 2003.

Gary Doore, *What Survives?: Contemporary Explorations of Life After Death.* New York: Tarcher, 1990.

Infinite Potential: The Life and Ideas of David Bohm. Directed by Paul Howard, CounterPoint Films, 2020. (available on YouTube)

www.reincarnationforum.com

Carol Bowman, *Children's Past Lives: How Past Life Memories Affect Your Child.* New York: Bantam, 1998.

Carol Bowman, *Return from Heaven: Beloved Relatives Reincarnated Within Your Family.* New York: HarperTorch, 2003.

Chapter 3

Tom Shroder, *Old Souls: Compelling Evidence from Children Who Remember Past Lives.* New York: Simon & Schuster, 1999.

Jim Tucker, MD, *Return to Life: Extraordinary Cases of Children Who Remember Past Lives.* New York: St. Martin's Griffin Press, 2015.

https://www.sfgate.com (*San Francisco Chronicle* website)

Ian Stevenson, MD, *Where Reincarnation and Biology Intersect.* Westport: Praeger, 1997.

Ian Stevenson, MD, *European Cases of the Reincarnation Type.* Jefferson: McFarland, 2008.

Jim Tucker, MD, *Before: Children's Memories of Previous Lives.* New York: St. Martin's Essentials, 2021.

Jodi Picoult, *the book of two ways.* New York: Ballantine Books, 2020 (a novel).

Journal of Near-Death Studies, https://link.springer.com/journal/10920/volumes-and-issues

Phaedo, Plato (428–347 B.C.E.)

Jim Tucker, MD, *Life Before Life: Children's Memories of Previous Lives.* New York: St. Martin's Press, 2005.

Raymond Moody, MD, (with Paul Perry), *Reunions: Visionary Encounters with Departed Loved Ones.* Ivy Books, 1994.

Morey Bernstein, *The Search for Bridey Murphy.* New York: Doubleday, 1989.

Rosemary Brown, *Unfinished Symphonies: Voices from the Beyond.* New York: William Morrow & Co., 1971.

Alan Greenhalgh, *Reincarnation and Misfortune in Old and Modern Japan.* lulu.com (self-published), 2017.

Trutz Hardo, *Children Who Have Lived Before: Reincarnation Today.* London: Random House UK, 2005.

Chapter 4

Jeffrey Furst, ed., *Edgar Cayce's Story of Jesus.* New York: Berkley Books, 1968.

W. H. Church, *Edgar Cayce's Story of the Soul.* Virginia Beach: A.R.E. Press, 1989.

Elaine Pagels, *Beyond Belief: The Secret Gospel of Thomas.* New York: Random House, 2003.

reincarnationforum.com

A Compendium of the Theological and Spiritual Writings of Emanuel Swedenborg. Boston: Crosby & Nichols, 1853.

Chapter 5

Deborah Blum, *Ghost Hunters: William James and the Search for Scientific Proof of Life after Death.* New York: Penguin Books, 2007.

N. Riley Heagerty, *Portraits from Beyond: The Mediumship of the Bangs Sisters*. White Crow Books, 2016.

whitecrowbooks.com

Andrew Jackson Davis, *The Principles of Nature, Her Divine Revelations, and a Voice to Mankind*. Emeryville: Andesite Press, 2015.

Barbara Weisberg, *Talking to the Dead: Kate and Maggie Fox and the Rise of Spiritualism*. New York: HarperOne, 2005 (reprint).

Gladys Osborne Leonard, *My Life in Two Worlds*. Time Life Education series, 1992.

Nandor Fodor, *Encyclopaedia of Psychic Science*. New York: Citadel, 1952.

https://thehauntedmuseum.com

https://www.insightsfromspirit.com

https://www.psychicsdirectory.com

https://swa.wildapricot.org (in the UK)

Sheila Ostrander and Lynn Schroeder, *Psychic Discoveries Behind the Iron Curtain*. Hoboken: Prentice-Hall, 1970 and 1997.

Russell Targ, *The Reality of ESP: A Physicist's Proof of Psychic Abilities*. Wheaton: Quest Books, 2012.

F. W. H. Myers, *Human Personality and the Survival of Bodily Death*. https://www.gutenberg.org/ebooks/38492.

Stephen Braude, *Immortal Remains: The Evidence of Life after Death*. Lanham: Rowman & Littlefield, 2003.

William Crookes, *The Quarterly Journal of Science*.

The Theosophist (journal, late 1800s)

H. P. Blavatsky, *The Secret Doctrine*. Pasadena: Theosophical University Press, 2014.

Carl Jung, *Psychology and the Occult*. Princeton: Princeton University Press, 1978.

Aniela Jaffé, *Was C. G. Jung a Mystic?: And Other Essays*. (Switzerland) Daimon Verlag, 1989.

Carl Jung, *Memories, Dreams, Reflections*. New York: Vintage, 1989.

Roger J. Woolger, PhD, *Other Lives, Other Selves: A Jungian Psychotherapist Discovers Past Lives*. New York: Doubleday, 1987.

Chapter 6

George Anderson, *We Don't Die: George Anderson's Conversations with the Other Side*. New York: Berkley, 1989.

Theresa Caputo, *You Can't Make This Stuff Up: Life-Changing Lessons from Heaven*. New York: Atria Books, 2015.

John Edward, *One Last Time: A Psychic Medium Speaks to Those We Have Loved and Lost*. New York: Berkley, 1998.

Jeffrey A. Wands, *Another Door Opens: A Psychic Explains How Those in the World of Spirit Continue to Impact Our Lives*. New York: Atria Books, 2007.

John Edward, *Crossing Over*. San Diego: Jodere Group, 2001.

Eileen Garrett, *Awareness*. Creative Age Press, 1943.

George Anderson, *Walking in the Garden of Souls*. New York: Berkley, 2002.

Carl Jung, *The Red Book*. New York: W. W. Norton & Company, 2009.

Chapter 7

Noël Coward, *Blithe Spirit*, (a stage play). London: Samuel French Ltd., 1968.

John Holland, *Bridging Two Realms*. Carlsbad: Hay House, 2018.

Carlos Castaneda, *Tales of Power*. New York: Simon & Schuster, 1974.

The I Ching, or Book of Changes. (Bollingen Series), Princeton: Princeton University Press, 1950.

Chapter 8

Archie E. Roy, *A Sense of Something Strange: Studies in the Paranormal*. (Scotland) Dog & Bone Press, 1990.

Gary Tillery, *The Seeker King: A Spiritual Biography of Elvis Presley*. Wheaton: Quest Books, 2013.

The Journal of The American Society for Psychical Research

Peter Manseau, *The Apparitionists: A Tale of Phantoms, Fraud, Photography and the Man Who Captured Lincoln's Ghost*. Boston: Houghton Mifflin Harcourt, 2017.

Clément Chéroux et al, *The Perfect Medium: Photography and the Occult*. New Haven: Yale University Press, 2005.

Christopher Bird, *The Divining Hand: The 500-Year-Old Mystery of Dowsing*. Atglen: Schiffer Publishing, 2000.

Alice A. Bailey, *Telepathy and the Etheric Vehicle*. New York: Lucis Publishing, 1971.

Patience Worth, *The Sorry Tale*. London: Forgotten Books, 2016.

H. J. Irwin and Caroline Watt, *An Introduction to Parapsychology*, Jefferson: McFarland, 2007.

http://www.skepdic.com (for The Skeptic's Dictionary)

https://www.oprah.com

Chapter 10

https://choprafoundation.org

https://www.catholic.org

https://www.hawking.org.uk

Body, Mind, Spirit Magazine (https://en.paperblog.com/body-mind-spirit/)

https://www.chabad.org

Alan Segal, *Life After Death: A History of the Afterlife in the Religions of the West*. New York: Doubleday, 2004.

Raymond A. Moody, Jr., MD, *Life After Life: The Investigation of a Phenomenon—The Survival of Bodily Death*. Mockingbird Books, 1975.

Chapter 13

Pierre Sichel, *Modigliani*. New York: E. P. Dutton, 1967.

William Fifield, *Modigliani: The Biography*. New York: William Morrow, 1976.

Charles Douglas, *Artist Quarter: Modigliani, Montmartre & Montparnasse*. London: Pallas Athene, 2018.

June Rose, *Suzanne Valadon: Mistress of Montmarte*. New York: St. Martin's Press, 1998.

www.theafterlifebook.com (for images taken by the author over six years)

Chapter 14

Brian L. Weiss, MD, *Many Lives, Many Masters.* New York: Simon & Schuster, 1988.

https://www.howstuffworks.com

https://www.telegraph.co.uk

www.afterliferesearch.org

https://www.myss.com

https://www.AmandaLinetteMeder.com

Chapter 15

W. H. Church, *Edgar Cayce's Story of the Soul.* Virginia Beach: A.R.E. Press, 1989.

Rupert Sheldrake, *Science and Spiritual Practices.* London: Coronet, 2017.

Carl B. Becker, *Paranormal Experience and Survival of Death.* Albany: State University of New York Press, 1993.

https://www.myss.com

www.theafterlifebook.com
www.thelanguageoftarot.com

*The following pages are here for you to make notes,
if the spirit so moves you.*

Appendix

GROUPS AND PUBLICATIONS

Groups

As I was researching the material for this book, I came across here and there the names of groups dedicated to the study of the unknown world. I'm listing these here. But I can also point out that if you go to Wikipedia and search for "spiritualist groups," you'll find a huge list of them around the world. Granted, this isn't a "filtered" list, so I don't know which is a great group and which isn't. This list was put together by the website, readersandrootworkers.org, and it includes thirty-four groups and ten spiritualist camps.

Here are some of the groups, though only a few still exist in the United States:

National Spiritualist Association of Churches (US)
The Elysium Psychic School (UK)
The College of Psychic Studies (UK)
Society for Psychical Research (UK)
The American Society for Psychical Research (US)
(Edgar Cayce's) Association for Research and Enlightenment (US)
Institut Métapsychique International (FR)
Rhine Research Center (US)
Parapsychology Foundation (US)
The Omega Institute for Holistic Studies (US)
Paranormal Research Forum (US)

Afterlife Research and Education Institute (US)
The Society for Scientific Exploration (US)
Arthur Findlay College (UK)
Foundation for Research on the Nature of Man (FRNM)
C. G. Jung Foundation (international)

Publications
This list sure doesn't include all the books out there today about ESP, channeling, and other kinds of spirit communication. These are just the books I've come across in my own reading.

An Experiment with Time (1927)
Extrasensory Perception (1934)
Irreducible Mind (2007)
The Journal of Parapsychology (science and scientists examine *psi*)
International Journal of Parapsychology
Journal of the Society for Scientific Exploration ("fringe science")
Mental Radio (author Upton Sinclair's psychic ability experiments with his wife)
Old Souls (a report on Dr. Ian Stevenson's past life research with children)
Parapsychology: Frontier Science of the Mind (reprinted 2010)
The Roots of Coincidence (the late author Arthur Koestler reviews paranormal events)
Journal of the Society for Psychical Research (UK)
The Journal of the American Society for Psychical Research (US)
Proceedings of the Society for Psychical Research
Encyclopaedia of Occultism and Parapsychology (2001)
Psychic News (1932 – July 2010)
Psi Review
The Journal of Religion and Psychical Research
Helix Press (issued by The Parapsychology Foundation, New York, New York)

Notes

Notes

Notes

Notes

Notes

Notes

Notes

Notes

Notes

Notes

Notes

Notes

Notes

Notes

Notes

Notes

Notes

Notes

Notes

Notes